baae

MADE IN INDIA. Copyright © Meera Sodha, 2015
Text on wine and Indian food copyright © Sunaina Sethi
Photography copyright © David Loftus
Design by Fig Tree

All rights reserved. Printed in China. For information, address
Flatiron Books, 175 Fifth Avenue, New York, N.Y. 10010.

www.flatironbooks.com

The Library of Congress Cataloging-in-Publication Data
is available upon request.

ISBN 978-1-250-07101-9 (paper over board)
ISBN 978-1-250-07102-6 (e-book)

Flatiron books may be purchased for educational, business, or promotional
use. For information on bulk purchases, please contact the Macmillan
Corporate and Premium Sales Department at 1-800-221-7945 extension
5442 or write to specialmarkets@macmillan.com.

Originally published in Great Britain by the Penguin Group.

First U.S. Edition: September 2015

10 9 8 7 6 5 4 3 2 1

MADE IN INDIA

Recipes from an
Indian Family Kitchen

MEERA SODHA

Photography by David Loftus

FLATIRON
BOOKS
NEW YORK

CONTENTS

ALTERNATIVE CONTENTS

For my mum, Nita Sodha

Introduction

An Indian kitchen can be anywhere in the world.

I've never lived in India, but I grew up in England eating the same food my ancestors have eaten for hundreds of years and which I still cook in my kitchen, every day.

My family's home cooking is unrecognizable from a lot of the food that is served up in most curry houses across the UK; ours is all at once simple, delicious, and fresh. Real Indian home cooking is largely an unknown cuisine, and it's my love for what we Indians really eat at home that has led me to share these recipes with you now.

My grandparents' kitchen started in Gujarat, where this story begins. Gujarat is the area north of Mumbai and south of Pakistan, with Rajasthan to the east and the Arabian Sea to the west. The Arabian Sea is where my grandfather, Mathuradas Lakhani, happened to be looking when his curiosity to find out what lay across it got the better of him. Along with his wife, his father and his brother, he set sail for Kenya to begin a life there, taking with him all the family recipes.

Africa back then was a land of opportunity for anyone with a good idea. He had many, and, along with his father and brother, he set up Kenya's first printing press, a Coca-Cola bottling factory and, later, when he moved to Uganda, a grain mill. With his new-found prosperity he employed a cook, and so my mother grew up not cooking, but being cooked for, until she arrived in England.

My family's arrival in England was sudden and part of a well-documented episode in British history. Idi Amin, tyrant, dictator, and then-president of Uganda, woke up one day in 1972 and gave all Asians living there 90 days' notice to leave the country before he would start to kill them. Along with thousands of others, my family left everything: their homes, businesses, money, and friends. They arrived in Lincolnshire with one suitcase between all five of them and £50 with which to start a new life.

While the backdrop to their lives changed in every way – the country itself, the language, the people, the culture, the weather, and local ingredients – their food did not. My grandparents went to work, and my mother reassembled our Indian kitchen in Lincolnshire and carried on cooking the family recipes.

She met my father, had me and my sister, and continued to cook, day in, day out, to feed her growing family, arranging whatever she could afford into various pots and pans to magical effect, conjuring up tastes and smells of the past and linking us, in an instant, to our ancestral home.

At the same time, she started to use local ingredients. Indian cooking can be adapted to any place by encompassing whatever ingredients are available. As we lived in Lincolnshire, a county that abounds in local produce, she was able to use gorgeous beets, rhubarb, and squash in her cooking, as well as fish from the nearby docks in Grimsby and local meat.

Whichever vegetables or meat she used, every day there would be fresh hot chapatis—made in minutes, gobbled in seconds. She would cook dishes so fragrant with cloves, cinnamon, and cumin that they'd make your mouth water and your belly rumble, and her sweetly spiced desserts filled the house with smells that would make you weak at the knees. All these dishes were cooked with love, instinct, and her trusty wooden spoon – the same spoon that she bought just days after arriving in the UK with barely a penny to her name.

My mother's spoon cast a spell over me from a young age, and it is to her that I owe my love of cooking. Using all the culinary knowledge that she passed on to me, I've created this collection of recipes so that you can make the same delicious, fresh-tasting food in your own home.

Some of the dishes in this book are ancient family recipes which have never been recorded or written down until now. They were passed down from woman to woman in our family, with easy-to-remember anecdotes for when cooking alone, with sayings such as "the mango should be as hard as a cricket ball" and the dough "as soft as your ear lobe," or "when the spoon sticks up in the mixture, it's ready." Many measurements were in "handfuls," "bowls," and unique boxes and cans.

Other recipes are my mother's, all of which apply Gujarati know-how and techniques to local ingredients. A couple of her recipes are Ugandan.

And a few are mine and have come into my kitchen (and heart) by way of friends, my travels far and wide across India, and my experimentation in the kitchen using Indian flavors.

Not everything in this book is a "curry" (a term I use loosely for dishes with sauce), and there are no set rules. Many dishes are frugal and thrifty, turning humble vegetables, pantry staples, and even leftovers into something delicious.

I hope this book will allow you to experience what we consider to be real home-cooked Indian food, and will also give you a greater understanding of different ingredients and techniques so that you can come up with your own recipes using your own instinct, with just a few key spices and whatever happens to be in your fridge.

On my last birthday, Mum passed her treasured wooden spoon over to me as a present. With it was a note that simply read, "Happy cooking." I hope, like that spoon, this book fills your kitchen with the same happiness as it has done ours.

A word on Indian cooking

Indian food has a reputation for being intimidating and complicated, but this is a myth. The majority of Indian home cooking is fresh, simple, and quick, and I'm on a mission to show you just how easy it is.

This book is written for everyone, from first-timers to seasoned cooks, and for those who love Indian food but don't know where to start.

Most of the recipes can be cooked quickly, in around 30 minutes, and you should be able to pick up the majority of ingredients in your local supermarket on the way home from work without having to go on a wild-goose chase (there are no wild-goose recipes in this book).

How to use this book

In order to help you, I've laid out a section that introduces you to Indian ingredients on page 286, explaining what each one tastes like and how to use it, along with shopping tips. There is also an Alternative Contents on page 6, which will help you to pick what to cook depending on the occasion or your mood, and there are some menu ideas on page 278.

My most important piece of advice to you, however, is this: taste everything.

Try your dish at the beginning, middle, and end. Add something, stir and taste, and if it's a spice or chili you're adding, add it little by little. The more you taste, the more you'll be able to understand your ingredients, how they behave, and what you enjoy.

A note on naming

Recipe titles and the names of spices are given in English, with translations in Gujarati and the odd adopted Hindi or Swahili word, unless the dish or spice is better known by its Indian name, in which case the translation is in English.

Kitchen equipment

Although there are many items specific to a traditional Indian kitchen, the truth is that very little special equipment is needed in order to get started. When I left home to come to London I took with me a spice tin, a sharp knife, a lidded pan, a saucepan, and a wooden spoon. I cooked in a kitchen the size of a phone booth. All went well – I'm still friends with the people I cooked dinner for back then – and I haven't added a huge amount of special equipment to my kitchen since.

You can easily get by on some basics which you are already likely to have.

The must-haves:

- A good knife, sharp enough to make cutting tomatoes enjoyable and easy.

- Some pans: a wide-bottomed frying pan with a lid, or two frying pans if you cook a lot. One with a tight clear lid is very useful when you're cooking rice (so that you can look in without letting the steam escape). A deep saucepan is essential, too.

- A rolling pin, if making breads. Indian rolling pins, "velans," are thin and light and easy to maneuver (see Recommended suppliers, page 309).

- A large, heavy mortar and pestle for crushing garlic, ginger, chilis, and bashing up spices.

- A pair of digital kitchen scales – especially helpful for making bread.

The nice-to-haves:

- A garlic press, for frequent garlic crushing.

- A chapati board (a patlo): inexpensive and available online (see Recommended suppliers, page 309), it will help you to roll perfect round chapatis because of its circular shape.

- A wooden chapati press: this small disc-shaped press has a short handle attached at one side, and allows you to press your chapatis and other breads so that they cook quickly and evenly.

- An electric spice grinder: although it does a similar job to a mortar and pestle, if you're cooking a lot it's worth the investment as it will transform whole spices and nuts into a fine powder in seconds. A wet and dry one will allow you to whizz up garlic, ginger, and chilis into a paste, too.

- An Indian spice tin (a masala dabba), to keep all your favorite spices fresh and at hand (see Recommended suppliers, page 309).

- A blender or food processor, for making light work of frequent tasks such as chopping vegetables and blending chutneys or tomatoes; especially useful when cooking in large quantities.

- An ice cream maker, if tempted by the recipes in this book. While you can always churn by hand, an ice cream maker does all the hard work for you. The small ones are relatively inexpensive to buy now, and make ice cream an easy and quick dessert to whip up.

Helpful weights and measures

General

1 teaspoon = $\frac{1}{3}$ of a tablespoon = 5ml

1 tablespoon = 3 teaspoons = 15ml

Rice and legumes

Appetites will vary (so plan accordingly), but as a general rule allocate 2 ounces (50–60g) of dry rice per person. As for legumes allow 4 ounces (100g) of the dried variety per person, or 7–8 ounces (200g) of soaked or canned.

Meat and fish

Around 5–7 ounces (150–200g) of meat or fish is a good amount per person for a main course, alongside other things such as bread or sides.

A good rule of thumb if you're using meat on the bone is to buy a third more than the weight of boneless meat given in a recipe. For example, if a recipe calls for 1¼ pounds (600g) of boneless meat, buy around 1¾ pounds (800g) of meat on the bone.

Spices

You might find the following measures helpful if grinding whole spices for powder.

Cardamom Approximately 12 pods = 1 teaspoon of ground cardamom

Cinnamon 1 1¾-inch stick = 1 teaspoon of ground cinnamon

Coriander 1 teaspoon of coriander seeds = 1½ teaspoons of ground coriander

Cumin 1 teaspoon of cumin seeds = 1¼ teaspoons of ground cumin

Black pepper 1 teaspoon of peppercorns = 1¾ teaspoons of ground pepper

Citrus fruit

1 lime = roughly 3 tablespoons (30ml) of juice

I lemon = roughly ¼ cup (50ml) of juice

Garlic

1 fat clove of garlic = 1 teaspoon of finely chopped garlic

Onions

1 large onion = approximately 7 ounces (200g)

Tomatoes

1 medium tomato = approximately 6 ounces (170g)

Eat like an Indian, think like an Indian

Without wanting to generalize too much, before you start to cook like an Indian, here's how to think like an Indian:

Eat with your hands, specifically the right. Eating with the left is taboo.

Always look like you're studying hard when your parents are around, no matter how old you are.

Never waste food. Offer it to neighbors, the postman, and the birds before putting it in the trash.

Always turn up an hour late for an event, or set the time of your event an hour early to ensure your guests arrive on time; this is called "Indian Time."

As an Indian host, you must feed your guests until they beg for mercy – it's the ultimate hospitality.

Feed the dog chapatis. Dogs love chapatis.

Believe that almonds have the power to increase your IQ, even if it has not been scientifically proven.

No matter how many people in your family, make sure everyone piles into the same car, whatever the length of your journey.

Spend at least an hour at the door when saying goodbye to people you're visiting.

Do not come back from India with baggage under the weight limit – it is a faux pas.

Treat cricket as the second religion.

Encourage your children to become lawyers, doctors, or engineers.

Make good Tupperware part of the family, and never waste a good container. Mum's chapati-flour tub is a Tupperware one from the 1990s.

Plastic wrap your remote control and don't take the covers off the sofa, no matter how many years you've had it.

Call any Indian woman older than you "Aunty," and any older man "Uncle."

Be naturally suspicious of any food that is not home-cooked. Always take your own food with you wherever you go, even if you're not going far.

Assess the suitability of your sister's or friend's new date by first asking how much they earn and what their parents do.

If one member of the family is going on vacation, gather the entire family to say goodbye at the airport.

Chapati Dog

STARTERS

01

& SNACKS

STARTERS AND SNACKS

Indians are always nibbling; in fact, India has one of the biggest street-food and snacking cultures in the world. With a lot of passion for food and very little regulation about who can sell food and where, streets thrum and resonate across the country with the calls of a thousand food hawkers selling their snacks. Whether it's from bikes turned into kitchens, from bins turned into ovens or from baskets perched on heads, food is sold everywhere.

In the far north in Amritsar you'll find lines of turbaned Sikhs waiting for the legendary Amritsari fish, a spiced deep-fried kingfish, and in the winter the mustard-seed curry "sarson ka saag," topped with freshly made butter and mopped up with cornbread. Travel down to Delhi and you'll see spiced potato tikki (see page 46), dressed with tamarind chutney, and delicious blackened kebabs served with "roomali roti" – chapatis as thin as hankies and as big as car wheels. In Mumbai, they love pav bhaji (see page 66), a rich mash of vegetables eaten with bread, chicken tikka (see page 36), and chaat (see page 43). Head east to Kolkata for a "kati roll" – an egg-fried wrap of meat or vegetables; west to Gujarat for some fluffy ondwa (see page 35) or addictive pea kachori (see page 22); and south for dosas, thin crispy pancakes made from rice and lentils.

What might have started out as an idea on the street can now be found in the homes of many Indians, recreating the famous dishes they first tried on a hot, dusty street corner and adding them to the snacks already served in their homes.

My favorites are the ubiquitous samosas (see page 48); the chili paneer (see page 27), which I first encountered near my grandparents' home in Leicester; and the corn on the cob (see page 32), which our family has eaten in the same way in Uganda, in India, and in Lincolnshire, where it grows as tall as me.

There is so much variety, the only tough decision you'll face is what to eat first.

PEA KACHORI
Pastry-encased cinnamon-spiced peas

These delicious balls of pea-green joy are an old Gujarati delicacy. They are often served at family functions because they're very easy to wolf down when no one is looking. Baked in the oven, they are best served on a bed of sharp lime-pickled onions (see page 221), alongside some mint and yogurt chutney (see page 219).

A food processor is ideal to make the kachori mixture, but if you don't have one, you can use a mortar and pestle and a potato masher. Amazingly, pea kachori can be made almost entirely from items you'll probably already have in the freezer and pantry.

MAKES AROUND 25 KACHORI (TO SERVE 5 TO 8 PEOPLE)

For the filling

1¾-inch piece of ginger, peeled and roughly chopped

2 fresh green chilis, roughly chopped (seeded if you prefer less heat)

1¼ pounds frozen petit pois or garden peas, defrosted

canola oil

1 teaspoon mustard seeds

1¼ teaspoons ground cinnamon

1¼ teaspoons garam masala

½ teaspoon ground turmeric

1¾ teaspoons salt (or to taste)

½ teaspoon chili powder

For the pastry

2 cups plus 2 tablespoons all-purpose flour, plus extra to dust

½ teaspoon salt

1½ tablespoons canola oil

¾ cup hot water

Preheat the oven to 350°F and lightly grease a tray with some oil.

Place the ginger and green chilis in a food processor and blitz into a paste, or bash them up using a mortar and pestle. If using a food processor, remove the paste and set to one side. Briefly blitz the peas in the food processor and set aside, or mash up using a potato masher.

Put 3 tablespoons of oil in a frying pan on medium heat and, when it's hot, add the mustard seeds. When they start to crackle, add the ginger and chili paste, stir-fry for a couple of minutes, then add the peas and cook for a further 5 minutes.

Now add the cinnamon, garam masala, turmeric, salt, and chili powder. Cook for a further 2 minutes, or until there is little to no moisture left but the peas are still bright green. Transfer to a bowl and put to one side.

To make the dough, put the flour in a bowl, make a well in the middle, and add the salt and oil. Rub through with your fingers until the flour resembles fine breadcrumbs. Pour in ½ cup of the water and add the rest little by little, kneading it into the dough until it feels nice and firm. Pour a teaspoon of oil into your hands and pat the dough with it to keep it moist.

Before rolling out the pastry, get your station ready. You will need a clean floured surface, a bowl of flour, and a rolling pin. Now pinch off a piece of dough roughly the size of a marshmallow. Dip your dough ball into the bowl of flour and roll into a circle roughly 4 inches in diameter (the size of a bottom of a mug). To speed things up, you can divide the dough into the small balls before rolling and stuffing them.

To make the kachori, pop a heaped teaspoon of pea mixture in the middle and bring the sides of the pastry up tightly around the peas. Seal the pastry at the top by pinching it closed, then pinch off any excess pastry, roll the kachori into a ball, and put it on a plate. Then make the rest. The first one you make might look a bit odd, so mark it out for tasting when it comes out of the oven.

Roll the kachori balls around on the baking tray to coat them in the oil and bake in the oven for 20 to 30 minutes, or until golden brown.

CHILI PANEER

Every now and then, when we were growing up, Mum would find me and my sister wherever we were hiding in the house, whip us into the car, and take us to Leicester on a sari shopping expedition. Our only consolation (aside from secretly unraveling beautifully folded saris in the shops) was a dish of freshly prepared chili paneer from one of the nearby food stalls or cafés afterwards.

This dish is as popular with kids as it is with grandparents. Here's Mum's recipe for this spectacular street food.

SERVES 4

1½ teaspoons cumin seeds
14 ounces paneer
canola oil
4 cloves of garlic, crushed
1 fresh green chili, very finely sliced
¾ teaspoon ground black pepper

1 teaspoon salt
1 tablespoon tomato paste
½ teaspoon sugar
4 scallions, finely sliced into rings
lemon wedges, to serve

Throw the cumin seeds into a mortar and pestle and roughly grind them to a coarse powder. Next cut the paneer into ¾-inch cubes. Pour a thin coating of oil into a large frying pan and bring it to a high heat. Fry the paneer in batches, turning the pieces until golden brown on each side, and transfer them to a dish lined with paper towels. Watch out, as the paneer may spit; if so, half cover the pan with a lid.

Put 2 tablespoons of oil into the pan, followed by the garlic, green chili, cumin, black pepper, and salt. Sauté for around 3 minutes on a low heat, stirring occasionally. Add the tomato paste and sugar and stir, then put the paneer back into the pan along with a splash of water. Cover the pan and simmer for a further 5 minutes.

Take the lid off the pan, add the scallions and simmer until there is no water left. Serve fresh and hot with a squeeze of lemon.

FIRE-SMOKED EGGPLANTS

Ringra nu orro

I used to bake my eggplants in the oven for this recipe, but after seeing my aunt smoke hers to perfection over a direct flame in her kitchen in Porbandar, I can't go back to my old ways. She holds the eggplant by its green stalk over the stove until the skin chars and the soft, creamy white flesh begins to peek through. Then she peels off the blackened skin and cooks the eggplant in a garlic and tomato sauce.

It's a gorgeously rich, smoky mash of flavors and one of my all-time favorite dishes. I eat it hot or cold with chapatis, chapati chips, or fresh naan.

SERVES 4 TO 6 AS A DIP

1¾-inch piece of ginger, peeled and roughly chopped

5 cloves of garlic, roughly chopped

1 fresh green chili, roughly chopped

salt

2 large eggplants

3 tablespoons canola oil (plus extra for brushing the eggplants with)

1 onion, finely chopped

2 medium ripe tomatoes, finely chopped

1 teaspoon ground cumin

1 teaspoon ground coriander

a small bunch of cilantro (½ ounce)

To serve

Greek yogurt

chapatis or chapati chips (see page 272)

Put the ginger, garlic, and chili into a mortar and pestle along with a pinch of salt, bash to a pulp, and set aside.

Pierce the eggplants in a few places with a sharp knife so that they don't explode when cooking, and lightly brush them with some oil. Hold them one by one with a pair of tongs over a naked flame on the stove. Keep turning them until the skin blackens and the eggplant collapses and goes floppy. This should take around 15 minutes for both eggplants.

When the eggplants are cool enough to handle, peel off the charred skin, scoop the flesh out into a bowl and mash using a fork, then set aside.

Put the oil into a wide-bottomed, lidded frying pan on a medium heat. When it's hot, fry the onion for 8 to 10 minutes, until soft and golden. Add the tomatoes, cover the pan and allow them to cook for another 4 to 5 minutes. Then add the ginger, garlic, and chili paste and leave to cook for a couple of minutes before adding the eggplant mash, cumin, ground coriander, and ¾ teaspoon of salt.

Cover the pan, and cook for a further 5 minutes until all the ingredients have come together into a lovely thick mash. Taste for salt and spice and adjust if necessary.

Chop the cilantro and stir into the mash, then serve in a large sharing bowl or in individual bowls with a dollop of yogurt on the top and some small chapatis or chapati chips on the side.

CORN ON THE COB WITH CHILI GARLIC BUTTER

Sekeli makai anna marchu

Corn has followed my family on our journey halfway across the world. It grew in Porbandar in India, where my grandma grew up; in Kampala, Uganda, where Mum grew up; and in Lincolnshire, where I grew up. We still eat it in the same way, no matter which country we're in: blistered on a fire until it becomes deliciously smoky, then slathered in chili butter with a squeeze of lime to finish. The garlic is my addition: I think it tastes great melted into spicy butter.

Try to buy your corn when it's as fresh as possible, and with husks if you're not eating it right away, as corn starts to deteriorate the moment it's been harvested. It should feel tender, bouncy to the touch, and juice easily when you press it.

SERVES 4

For the chili garlic butter

½ cup salted butter

4 fat cloves of garlic, crushed

1 fresh red chili, very finely chopped

a little salt, if need be

4 fresh ears of corn

1 lime, quartered

To make the chili garlic butter, cut the butter into cubes and put it into a small pan on a gentle heat. When it's melted, add the garlic and chili, stir, and leave to cook for around 5 minutes, then pour into a bowl. Leave to one side to cool down.

Take the corn out of the fridge around 10 to 15 minutes before cooking to get it to room temperature. Pull out any silk, as it can catch on fire when cooking.

Turn the gas burner to a medium to high flame and, taking one of the cobs, hold it over the heat with a pair of tongs. Rotate it every 30 seconds until the kernels start to blacken and char. If it starts to pop, turn the heat down a little bit and carry on. It should take around 5 to 6 minutes to cook each cob.

Keep the cooked corn warm by wrapping each ear tightly in foil until you're ready to eat. Serve with the chili garlic butter spooned over the top, a sprinkle of salt, and a squeeze of lime.

Tip: I love to make a big batch of this chili garlic butter and keep it in the fridge so I can add a spoonful to whatever I'm cooking.

ONDWA
Semolina bread with spiced vegetables

The ultimate Gujarati all-in-one snack, ondwa is a type of bread made with yogurt and semolina, studded with vegetables, and topped with a layer of glimmering mustard seeds and sesame seeds. In Gujarati households it's pretty much expected that you have a running supply of ondwa in your fridge in case friends or family pop by (although all the better for you if they don't).

This recipe benefits from the savory taste of older yogurt, to give it a slightly sour tang, so the longer you've had yours, the better.

MAKES 12 PORTIONS

For the ondwa

2 tablespoons canola oil
   (plus extra to grease the cake pan)
1¾ cups coarse semolina
1 cup whole-milk yogurt
1 zucchini (7 ounces), grated
2 medium carrots (6 ounces in total), grated
½ cup green peas
1 onion, finely chopped
1¾-inch piece of ginger, peeled and finely grated
½ teaspoon ground turmeric

½ teaspoon chili powder
¾ teaspoon salt
1½ teaspoons baking powder
½ cup water

For the tarka

2 tablespoons canola oil
1 fresh red chili, finely chopped
1 tablespoon sesame seeds (plus extra
   to sprinkle)
½ tablespoon mustard seeds (plus extra
   to sprinkle)

Preheat the oven to 400°F and lightly grease a 9 x 11-inch cake pan with oil.

Put the semolina into a large bowl, pour in 2 tablespoons of oil and mix together. Add the yogurt, zucchini, carrots, peas, onion, ginger, turmeric, chili powder, salt, and baking powder. Mix thoroughly.

Pour in ⅓ cup of the water, then add the rest little by little, until the batter takes on a thick, custard-like consistency. Taste the mixture – although it will be raw, it will give you a good idea of salt and chili seasoning – and adjust if necessary.

To make the tarka (the spice-infused oil), heat the oil in a pan and, when it's hot, add the chili, sesame seeds, and mustard seeds. When the mustard seeds start to pop, carefully pour into the batter and stir.

Pour the batter into the cake pan, sprinkle generously with sesame seeds and mustard seeds and bake in the oven for 35 minutes, or until cooked. The usual test applies to check if it's done: if you insert a knife and it comes out clean, the ondwa is ready.

Leave to cool before taking it out of the pan and cutting (it will be much easier). Enjoy either warmed up or cold with some cilantro chutney (see page 212) and a hot cup of chai (see page 260). Store in an airtight container in the fridge and eat within 3 days.

OVEN-ROASTED CHICKEN TIKKA *Murghi na tikka*

The chicken tikka you find in restaurants is normally so luminously orange you could see it from space. Our family recipe is much tastier and nowhere near as brightly colored. We use chicken thighs, which are nice and juicy, and dress our chicken tikka with a sharp mint and yogurt chutney (see page 219). If you fancy something fresh on the side, my chaat salad (see page 192) is perfect.

If you have any leftovers, chicken tikka is great in sandwiches and wraps with a bit of cucumber, tomato, onion, and chutney. Or you could always make some chicken tikka masala. Skewers aren't necessary, but they look nice and help divide quantities. If you use them, soak them in advance to avoid burning them in the oven.

SERVES 4 TO 6

canola oil

1¼ pound skinless, boneless chicken thighs

1¾-inch piece of ginger, peeled and roughly chopped

4 cloves of garlic, roughly chopped

1 fresh green chili, roughly chopped

salt

½ cup whole-milk yogurt

½ teaspoon chili powder

½ teaspoon ground turmeric

¾ teaspoon cumin seeds, crushed

¾ teaspoon sugar

1 teaspoon sweet paprika

1 teaspoon garam masala

Preheat the oven to 400°F. Line two oven trays with parchment paper and coat them with a very thin layer of oil.

Pick the chicken thighs over to remove any excess fat, then chop into small pieces, around 1 x ¾ inch, and set to one side in a bowl.

Using a mortar and pestle, bash the ginger, garlic, and green chili with a pinch of salt until it turns into a paste. Add the paste to the chicken pieces, followed by the rest of the ingredients and 1¼ teaspoons of salt (or to taste). Mix thoroughly and cover. Leave to marinate for at least 15 minutes and up to a few hours (the longer the better).

Shake any excess marinade off the chicken (or else you'll end up with a curry) and distribute the chicken between the two oven trays, so that you don't crowd them. Cook for around 20 minutes, turning the pieces over after 10 minutes so that they cook evenly.

Serve the chicken tikka with some salad leaves or chaat salad, and drizzle with mint and yogurt chutney.

PAN-FRIED CHICKEN LIVERS IN CUMIN BUTTER MASALA

Jeeru wari kalegi

Quick to make, these utterly delicious chicken livers are a great snack or starter. My grandfather used to wash these down with a glass of local Ugandan whisky after he came back from work at the grain mill.

The key to this dish is to use a hot frying pan initially so that the livers are crispy on the outside but not overcooked; they should be just blushing on the inside. They are delicate things which absorb the buttery flavors beautifully, so be gentle with them.

SERVES 4

9 ounces chicken livers

2 tablespoons unsalted butter

3 cloves of garlic, crushed

½ teaspoon cumin seeds

½ teaspoon salt (or to taste)

½ teaspoon ground black pepper

First pick over the livers and make sure they're well trimmed. Remove any sinewy bits and pat dry with a paper towel.

Melt the butter in a frying pan on a high heat. Once it's foaming and the pan is nice and hot, add the chicken livers and sear them for 1 to 2 minutes on each side until golden brown.

Turn the heat down to medium and add the garlic, cumin, salt, and pepper. Stir-fry for a minute, then add 2 tablespoons of water. Cover with a lid and simmer for a further 2 minutes, as this will ensure the chicken livers are cooked through without burning the garlic and spices. Take the lid off the pan and allow to simmer and reduce for up to 5 minutes, but no longer.

Serve with hot chapatis (see page 196), tomato chutney (see page 218), and kachumbar (see page 185), or some salad leaves. Local whisky optional.

CHANA KA CHIPS
Spicy roasted chickpeas

These crispy, roasted chickpeas are addictive, quick to make, and even quicker to polish off. In India they are made by smashing the chickpeas flat and leaving them to dry in the sun before spicing. In England our less favorable weather calls for oven-baking.

This is a great secret pantry snack to have up your sleeve when you want something to keep you company through a couple of episodes of your latest box set or a romantic comedy. Chickpeas don't judge.

SERVES 4

2 14-ounce cans of unsalted chickpeas (salted are fine as long as you adjust the salt in the recipe accordingly)

4 tablespoons canola oil

1½ teaspoons salt

1 teaspoon chili powder

2 teaspoons ground cumin

Preheat the oven to 400°F and make sure your oven racks are in the middle of the oven.

Pour the chickpeas into a colander, rinse with water, and shake dry. Pop them into a bowl and add the oil, salt, chili powder, and cumin, then mix thoroughly until all the chickpeas are evenly coated.

Spread the chickpeas in an even layer on two oven trays and bake until crisp, for around 30 minutes, shaking them every 10 minutes to ensure they bake evenly and don't burn.

CHILI-ROASTED CASHEWS
Masala wara kaju

Cashews really do make a valiant journey in order to reach us in those neat little bags. They're harvested by hand from their tall trees, then separated from their fruits, the cashew apples, under which the nuts grow. They are soaked and roasted to remove the toxic acid in their shells, then cleaned, dried, and transported across many oceans to get to our shops. That's the hard part. The easy part is this, the recipe for making your cashews super tasty.

SERVES 4

7 ounces unsalted cashew nuts
1 tablespoon canola oil
½ teaspoon salt

1 teaspoon chili powder
ground black pepper

Preheat the oven to 325°F.

Line a large roasting tray with foil and throw the cashews onto it, so that they are all on a level playing field. Put the cashews into the oven to roast for 6 to 8 minutes. You are looking for a nice light golden color, but no darker than that.

When they're done, take them out of the oven and transfer them to a bowl. Add the oil and, using a spoon to mix, ensure all the nuts are coated before adding the salt and chili powder. Mix again and throw in a few twists of the pepper mill to your desired taste.

Resisting the temptation to eat them immediately, leave them to cool down completely so that they crisp up nicely.

PAPADUM CHAAT
Aloo papad chaat

Blaring bhangra music. Crazy rickshaw drivers. Pinks. Oranges. Blues. Heady spices. Smiling people everywhere. My first trip to Delhi was an explosion of smells, colors, and sounds. This recipe is my reinvention of the city's famous street food, aloo papdi chaat, and it's Delhi in a bite. From earthy chickpeas to juicy pomegranate jewels, spicy potatoes, lime, and tangy chutneys, each mouthful is a festival of Indian flavors.

The recipe requires a fair bit of prepping of ingredients, but you can make the chutneys and the potato, chickpea, and onion mixture in advance, then throw everything else together really quickly, just before eating.

SERVES 4

date and tamarind chutney (see page 216)

mint and yogurt chutney (see page 219)

4 medium-sized new potatoes

1 14-ounce can of black chickpeas (kala chana), although white will do

1 red onion, very finely diced

½ teaspoon chili powder

½ teaspoon salt

6 to 8 papadums (either cooked or uncooked)

a big bunch of cilantro (1½ ounces)

4 ounces sprouted beans, bought or home-made (see page 271)

2 ounces thin sev (see page 308)

seeds of ½ pomegranate

½ lime, to serve

First, make the chutneys; this shouldn't take longer than 10 minutes.

Next, boil the potatoes in some salted water until just tender (when they fall off a knife easily). Drain them, rinse in cold water, and drain again. When cool enough to handle, chop them into large cubes and put them into a bowl. Drain and rinse the chickpeas and add them to the bowl, along with the onion, chili powder, and salt. Then mix.

If you're using uncooked papadums, heat a dry frying pan until hot and toast each papadum on both sides for 15 seconds, pressing down on them with a slotted spoon to cook them evenly. Put to one side.

To make the papadum chaat, finely chop the cilantro. Then scatter the chickpea, potato, and onion mixture on a serving plate, followed by the sprouted beans. Dot the plate generously with the date and tamarind chutney, then the mint and yogurt chutney, and sprinkle over the sev, cilantro, and pomegranate seeds.

Squeeze over the lime and serve alongside the papadums. Encourage everyone to scoop up the chaat using the papadums.

ROYAL BENGAL FISH FINGERS

There are a few streets in east London where, if you walk down them around dinner time, you can catch the smell of Bengali home cooking. It comes from the special Bengali mix of spices "panch phoran," or "five spice," made up of fennel seeds, nigella seeds, cumin, mustard, and fenugreek seeds. If you ever go to Kolkata, once the capital of the British Raj, you can pick up the same smell there around the same time of day, linking London and Bengal in one deep sniff.

This recipe is by no means traditional, but it's a happy marriage of both cities, nevertheless. A coffee or spice grinder is ideal for grinding the spices, but a mortar and pestle is a fair substitute.

SERVES 4 TO 6

canola oil
2 teaspoons fennel seeds
2 teaspoons cumin seeds
2 teaspoons mustard seeds
2 teaspoons nigella seeds
1 teaspoon fenugreek seeds
3 tablespoons all-purpose flour
1 tablespoon chickpea flour (besan)
2 teaspoons chili powder
6 cloves of garlic, crushed
2½-inch piece of ginger, peeled and grated

1½ teaspoons salt
4 eggs
1¼ pounds salmon or any firm white fish fillet, skinned and boned

For the breadcrumbs

3 cups breadcrumbs, either homemade (from stale bread) or bought
zest of 1 lemon
2 tablespoons finely chopped cilantro
salt

Preheat the oven to 400°F and lightly grease a baking tray with oil.

Next make the breadcrumbs. Put them on a shallow plate and add the lemon zest, cilantro, and a pinch of salt, then mix thoroughly. Put to one side.

To prepare the batter, grind the fennel, cumin, mustard, nigella, and fenugreek seeds to a powder in a coffee grinder or a mortar and pestle. Put the flours into a bowl and add the ground spices, chili powder, garlic, ginger, and salt, and mix thoroughly. In a separate bowl, beat the eggs together using a fork and whisk them into the flour mixture little by little.

Cut the fish into strips around ¾ inch wide and 3 inches long.

Now get your production line ready. Have your fish in front of you, followed by the spiced batter and finally the breadcrumbs. Take a piece of fish, dip it in the batter, allow any excess to drip off, then place it in the breadcrumbs, coating it all over. Repeat with the rest of the fish.

Transfer the fish fingers to the baking tray and bake them for 12 to 15 minutes, or until cooked through. Serve with baked masala fries (see page 176) and tomato chutney (see page 218), or as a Royal Bengal fish finger sandwich, for the ultimate cultural marriage.

SPICED POTATO TIKKI
Aloo tikki

While potato tikki might sound like a dance move, it is in fact a very popular street snack in India. The potatoes are mashed, spiced with onions, chili, lemon juice, and garam masala, and shallow-fried in rounds, just long enough to get a lovely golden crust on the outside. Dunk them into a paper plate with date and tamarind chutney (see page 216) or mint and yogurt chutney (see page 219) to eat your tikki like a real Indian.

MAKES AROUND 24 TIKKIS (TO SERVE 4 TO 6 PEOPLE)

1 pound potatoes (Yukon Gold, all-purpose)

2-inch piece of ginger, peeled and roughly chopped

1 fresh green chili, roughly chopped

salt

2 tablespoons canola oil (plus extra for frying the tikki)

1 teaspoon cumin seeds

1 large red onion, finely chopped

½ teaspoon chili powder

1 teaspoon garam masala

2 tablespoons all-purpose flour (plus extra for coating the tikkis)

½ cup garden peas (frozen are fine)

juice of ½ lemon

3 tablespoons chopped cilantro

Peel the potatoes and cut them into equal chunks. Place in a pan with a lid, cover with cold water, put the lid on, and bring them to a boil, then reduce to a simmer. When tender (when a knife pierces them easily), drain them and mash with a potato masher. Put them to one side.

Using a mortar and pestle, bash the ginger and the green chili along with a pinch of salt into a coarse paste and put to one side.

Put oil into a large frying pan on a medium heat and, when it's hot, add the cumin seeds and the chopped onion. Fry for 6 to 8 minutes, then add the ginger and chili paste, a teaspoon of salt, the chili powder, and the garam masala, and stir-fry for a couple of minutes.

Next add the mashed potato and flour, stir to mix, then add the peas, lemon juice, and cilantro. Mix thoroughly and cook for a further 2 to 3 minutes or until the peas are tender. Take off the heat and put to one side until cool enough to handle.

Prepare a bowl of flour to coat the tikkis with. When the mixture has cooled, take a bit of it and roll it into a golf ball shape. Flatten it out to make a patty and dip it into the flour to lightly coat. To check for seasoning, heat a teaspoon of oil in a frying pan and, when it's hot, fry the tikki for 3 minutes on each side or until brown and crispy. Remove with a slotted spoon. Adjust the seasoning as necessary, then make up the rest of the patties. Fry them in batches (around 6 at a time), so as not to overcrowd the pan. To keep the fried ones warm you can always put them in the oven on a low heat (250°F) until you are ready to serve them.

SCALLOPS WITH TAMARIND
Ambli wara scallops

Tamarind is often used with seafood on the Konkan coast, which runs south of Mumbai through Goa and into Kerala. It's a tangy, strong flavor, but used sparingly it combines very well with the natural sweetness in seafood.

For this recipe, I rely on fresh scallops, which are abundant in the North Sea. Any super fresh scallops work well here and there's no better way to cook them than with a little bit of tamarind.

SERVES 4

2 fat cloves of garlic, roughly chopped

¾ teaspoon salt

2 teaspoons tamarind paste

2½ teaspoons sugar

½ teaspoon chili powder

2 tablespoons canola oil

12 decent-sized scallops

1 tablespoon unsalted butter

With a mortar and pestle, bash the garlic and the salt together into a smooth paste. Put the paste into a bowl and add the tamarind, sugar, chili powder, 2 teaspoons of water, and the oil. Stir with a fork until well mixed. Toss the scallops in the marinade so they're evenly coated.

Place a non-stick frying pan on a high heat, put the butter into the pan, and coat the bottom of the pan with it. When the butter starts to foam, add 6 scallops (unless you can fry all 12 without overcrowding the pan) and fry for around 3 to 4 minutes. Try not to move them if you can help it, as that way they will develop a nice golden-brown edge. Turn them over and fry them for another 3 to 4 minutes.

Remove them from the pan with a slotted spoon, add more butter if need be, then fry the second batch. Serve alongside some fresh salad leaves.

THREE WAYS WITH SAMOSAS

These magic triangles have been with us through thick and thin. We celebrated with them after my sister got married, I cooked a batch up for everyone when I left my last job, and my mum makes them every year for the local village fête.

The usual Indian way with samosas is to stuff them with a mix of spicy potatoes, peas and carrots, or ground lamb, but my favorite fillings use really big handfuls of fresh herbs and local vegetables like beets (which work very well with feta).

I bake my samosas, using filo dough, rather than frying them, which means they're lighter and less oily, but just as delicious (and quicker to make).

It's worth mentioning that these are a great option if you're feeding crowds as they can be made in advance and frozen. Follow the instructions on page 52 on how to fill, fold, and bake your samosas.

Beet and feta samosas

MAKES 18 TO 24 SAMOSAS

14 ounces fresh beets

7 ounces feta cheese, cut into ¼-inch cubes

4 scallions, finely chopped

a medium bunch of cilantro (1 ounce), finely chopped

1 fresh green chili, finely chopped

4 cloves of garlic, crushed

½ teaspoon chili powder

1 teaspoon toasted cumin seeds, crushed

1 teaspoon garam masala

¾ teaspoon salt (or to taste)

Boil the beets until they become tender (this normally takes around 1 hour, depending on their size). To see if they're done, stick a sharp knife into them: they shouldn't resist the knife if cooked through. If you don't have the time, you could make these with pre-cooked beets (although what you gain in time you lose in taste).

Drain the beets and cool under a cold tap, peel off the skin, and mash roughly using a potato masher. Add the mash to a hot pan and stir-fry on a medium heat for 5 minutes to remove some of the moisture. The mash shouldn't be too wet as you want nice dry, crispy samosas. Take off the heat and transfer to a large bowl.

Add the feta cheese, scallions, cilantro, green chili, garlic, chili powder, cumin, garam masala, and salt. Mix, taste, then adjust any seasonings as you wish, but make sure that it is packed full of flavor, as you will lose some of the intensity when you cover it with the filo dough.

Chicken and coriander samosas

MAKES 18 TO 24 SAMOSAS

2 tablespoons canola oil
1 large onion, very finely chopped
1 tablespoon coriander seeds, crushed
1 fresh red chili, finely chopped
1 pound ground chicken (or turkey)
½ teaspoon cumin seeds, crushed
1 teaspoon chili powder

1 teaspoon garam masala
1-inch piece of ginger, peeled and grated
3 cloves of garlic, crushed
juice of ½ lemon
1 teaspoon salt (or to taste)
a medium bunch of cilantro (1 ounce),
   finely chopped

Place a frying pan on a medium heat and, when it's nice and hot, pour in the oil. Fry the onion for 6 to 8 minutes, or until it's just softening but not brown, as you still want a bit of a bite to it. Add the crushed coriander seeds, followed by the fresh red chili and the ground chicken.

Cook, stirring every now and again, for around 10 minutes, then add the rest of the spices: the cumin, chili powder, and garam masala. Stir, and follow with the ginger, garlic, lemon juice, and salt.

Keep cooking until the chicken is starting to brown, then take off the heat. Leave to cool until it is safe to handle, then add the cilantro. Taste and adjust the seasoning if necessary, then set aside.

Lamb and mint samosas

MAKES 18 TO 24 SAMOSAS

2 tablespoons canola oil
1 teaspoon cumin seeds
2 onions, finely diced
4 cloves of garlic, crushed
1 pound lean ground lamb
1½ teaspoons ground cumin

1 teaspoon ground coriander
1 teaspoon garam masala
2 tablespoons finely grated ginger
½ teaspoon chili powder
1 teaspoon salt (or to taste)
4 tablespoons finely chopped fresh mint

Put the oil into a large saucepan on a medium heat and, when it's hot, add the cumin seeds and fry for a minute. Add the onions and fry them for 8 to 10 minutes, until they're golden, then add the garlic and stir-fry for another couple of minutes.

Next, add the ground lamb, breaking it up with your wooden spoon to allow it to cook evenly. After 8 to 10 minutes, add the ground cumin, coriander, garam masala, ginger, chili, and salt.

Keep cooking until the lamb is starting to brown. Transfer the mix to another dish to cool, and add the mint leaves just before you make the samosas.

How to make samosas

MAKES 18 TO 24

12 to 16 sheets filo dough (approximately ½ pound), fresh or defrosted according to package instructions.

½ cup unsalted butter, melted
canola oil, to coat the oven tray

Preheat the oven to 400°F.

Delicately unroll one sheet of dough and place on a large cutting board. Brush it lightly with melted butter and layer with another sheet of filo dough. Cut the sheets horizontally into three strips (around 4 x 10 inches), using a sharp knife.

Make a cone shape at one side of the strip, place about 1 heaped tablespoon of the filling inside the cone, and fold the open side of the cone into the rest of the filo strip to cover and seal it. You should have a triangle shape now. Keep folding over the rest of the dough around the shape of the cone until you come to the end of the strip.

Cut off any excess dough, stick the strip down with a brush of melted butter and push on the seal with your fingers. Repeat.

To bake your samosas, brush them on both sides with butter and place on a lightly oiled baking tray in the center of the oven for 15 minutes.

If you don't want to bake your samosas right away, put them in a single layer on a non-stick surface and put them in the freezer. (Once frozen you can pile them all in a container or a freezer bag to save on space.)

To cook from frozen, brush both sides with butter and place on a lightly greased baking tray. Bake for 20 to 25 minutes or until golden.

Tip: If you're making different types of samosas, you can mark them out by sprinkling cumin seeds, sesame seeds, or nigella seeds on the top.

VEGETABLES

02

VEGETABLES

While I am not a vegetarian, I easily could be. India's vegetarian food shows you the giddy heights of what can be achieved when you take meat out of the mealtime equation.

Indian vegetarian dishes are the star of the show for the majority of Indians in India.

India is a vegetable paradise and there are countless vegetarian dishes available. Normally what ends up in the pot is whatever grows locally, according to the season. My grandma grew up cooking with vegetables native to the agriculturally rich Gujarat. Some local specialties included bottle gourds, bitter melons, cluster beans, cassava, guar beans, plantains, and wild garlic, as well as the many common vegetables we can find readily in our own supermarkets, like eggplant, potatoes, and cauliflower.

Dinner time for my grandma would consist of up to three vegetable dishes such as bateta nu shaak (a simple potato curry – see page 63), bhinda (okra), and kobi nu shaak (simply spiced spring cabbage – see page 80), all eaten with millet flatbread, chapatis, or rice. As in a lot of cuisines around the world, these rustic dishes may not be elaborate but they are packed full of flavor and, over the years, have become established regional and family favorites.

Coming to England, my mother and grandma started cooking with whatever was fresh and available. As they lived in Lincolnshire, England's biggest agricultural county, regular village activities included conversations about what to do with a bountiful crop of zucchini or nipping down to the farm shop to see if the beets had arrived.

With such a rich abundance of local vegetables over the years, our family repertoire has grown to include red peppers (red pepper and paneer curry – see page 76), butternut squash (roasted butternut squash curry – see page 61), green beans, asparagus, and leeks (sautéed spring vegetables with spices – see page 79).

Our treatment of vegetables has changed, too. Using such fresh produce with a real richness of flavor means there's little need to complicate things. Instead we treat vegetables lightly, plumping for wilted spinach, carrots that still have a bit of a crunch. Vegetables cooked just long enough to taste delicious yet still retain their goodness.

I may be pushing a (metaphorical) elephant up a Himalayan mountain by trying to get people to treat vegetables as main courses when they think about Indian food, but I consider it a challenge worth taking on. If I can get one chicken tikka masala fan to contemplate an evening spent with a chana masala, I'll see that as a battle half won.

EGGPLANT AND CHERRY TOMATO CURRY

Ringra tametar nu shaak

You can do all sorts of wonderful things with an eggplant, which is why an Indian kitchen is rarely without one. This eggplant curry was one of the first curries my mother ever taught me to cook, and although I've adapted it slightly to include cherry tomatoes because I enjoy their sweetness, it's still one of my most frequently cooked dishes during the week.

Make sure you have some nice thick yogurt on hand to eat with this curry, and some hot fluffy naan (see page 199).

SERVES 4

3 tablespoons canola or peanut oil

1 large onion, chopped

1 fresh green chili, finely chopped

1¾-inch piece of ginger, peeled and finely grated

4 cloves of garlic, crushed

10–11 ounces cherry tomatoes (around 30), halved

1½ teaspoons salt

½ teaspoon ground turmeric

1½ teaspoons ground cumin

1½ teaspoons ground coriander

2 tablespoons tomato paste

1 teaspoon sugar

2 large eggplants, quartered, then cut into ⅛-inch-thick pieces

Put the oil into a wide-bottomed, lidded frying pan on a medium heat. When it's hot, add the onion and cook for 6 to 8 minutes, until soft, translucent, and turning golden. Add the green chili, the ginger, and the garlic, and cook for a further 3 to 4 minutes, stirring frequently, before adding the halved cherry tomatoes, then put the lid on the pan and wait for the tomatoes to soften (this should take around 10 minutes).

Stir in the salt, turmeric, cumin, coriander, tomato paste, and sugar. Mix together, and when the mixture is looking paste-like add ⅔ cup of warm water, followed by the eggplant. Carefully coat the eggplant in the tomato mixture and pop the lid back on the pan.

Cook for around 15 to 20 minutes, on a low to medium heat, until the eggplant is tender, falling apart, and soft enough to cut with a wooden spoon.

Check for spices and salt and adjust as necessary, then serve with a spoonful of yogurt, a sprinkle of coriander, and a pile of naan.

ROASTED BUTTERNUT SQUASH CURRY WITH GARLIC AND TOMATOES

Lasan, tametar anna kaddu nu shaak

The squash family is an Indian cook's best friend. Squashes hold their shape in curries, they love a bit of chili, and you can usually feed a whole family using just one.

Although squash (like pumpkin) is popular in India, it's rarely roasted because the average kitchen in India does not have an oven. Roasting the squash gives it a caramelized and crispy skin, which works wonders with the tomatoes and garlic in this curry. This dish is complete with some golden garlic raita (see page 178) spooned over the top.

SERVES 4

1 large butternut squash (around 2¼ pounds), unpeeled, halved, seeded, then cut into ¾-inch-thick slices

4 tablespoons canola oil

salt

ground black pepper

1¼-inch piece of ginger, peeled and roughly chopped

4 cloves of garlic, roughly chopped

1 fresh green chili, roughly chopped

1 large onion, finely diced

14-ounce can of good-quality plum tomatoes

½ teaspoon sugar

1½ teaspoons ground coriander

1½ teaspoons ground cumin

Preheat the oven to 400°F and line two roasting trays with foil.

Throw the squash pieces onto both the roasting trays. Trickle over 2 to 3 tablespoons of oil and season generously with salt and black pepper. Toss together and bake for 30 minutes, or until they are soft and browning, turning halfway through.

Meanwhile, put the ginger, garlic, green chili, and a pinch of salt into a mortar and pestle and bash to a smooth paste. Set aside.

Put 1 tablespoon of oil into a frying pan on a medium heat. When it's hot, fry the onion for 8 to 10 minutes, until golden, and add the ginger, garlic, and chili paste. Cook for around 2 to 3 minutes, then tip in the can of tomatoes, breaking them up with a wooden spoon.

Cook for around 12 minutes, stirring occasionally, until the sauce is rich and thick. Add the sugar, coriander, cumin, ½ teaspoon of black pepper, and season with salt. Leave to cook for another 5 minutes, adding a little bit of water to get a good saucy consistency. Take the butternut squash out of the oven when ready and fold into the sauce. Serve with golden garlic raita and some fresh hot naan (see page 199) to mop it up with.

100 GARLIC-CLOVE CURRY

Lasan nu shaak

This recipe could otherwise be named "an insight into the mind of an addict." I am a garlic lover; I eat it raw, pickled, sliced, crushed, minced, fried, puréed, and roasted. Although this recipe appears to call for an excessive amount of fresh garlic, when cooked like this its strong punch gives way to something shockingly mild, delicate, and soft.

SERVES 2 AS A MAIN DISH OR 4 AS A SIDE

3 tablespoons canola oil

¾ teaspoon mustard seeds

10 fresh curry leaves

100 cloves of garlic (around 11 ounces, or 8 heads of garlic), peeled

½ teaspoon salt

½ teaspoon chili powder

1 teaspoon ground turmeric

1 teaspoon tamarind paste

½ cup coconut milk

Put the oil into a large, lidded pan on a medium heat and, when it's hot, add the mustard seeds. When they start to pop, add the curry leaves and the cloves of garlic.

Stir-fry for a couple of minutes to briefly sear the cloves on either side, then turn the heat down low, add ½ cup of warm water, and cover with the lid. You want the garlic to go soft and translucent, which will take around 15 to 20 minutes, but keep checking it to ensure the cloves don't burn. Add another splash of water if you think they're looking dry.

When the cloves are translucent they'll also be soft, so be careful not to stir them too much as you don't want to break them up. Add the salt, spices, and the tamarind paste, gently stir, and pop the lid on for another couple of minutes to cook through, then add the coconut milk. Stir gently again and cook for another 5 minutes.

Serve with naan (see page 199), but not with garlic naan. For tips on what to do with leftover coconut milk, see page 277.

BATETA NU SHAAK
Gujarati potato curry

This simple curry is an all-time Gujarati classic and has made it on to our list of top-five family dishes. Although humble, these soft potatoes submerged in a lightly spiced hot tomato sauce are a much-sought-after home comfort.

SERVES 4

6 large potatoes

3 tablespoons peanut oil

½ teaspoon mustard seeds

½ teaspoon cumin seeds

1¼-inch piece of ginger, peeled and grated

1 fresh green chili, finely chopped

1 7-ounce can of plum tomatoes

½ teaspoon ground turmeric

½ teaspoon chili powder

2 teaspoons ground coriander

2 teaspoons ground cumin

1 teaspoon sugar

1 teaspoon salt

a small bunch of fresh cilantro (½ ounce), finely chopped, to serve

Peel and cut the potatoes into 1-inch cubes.

Put the oil into a medium-sized, lidded frying pan on a medium heat. When it's hot, add the mustard seeds and cumin seeds. When the seeds crackle, add the ginger and green chili and stir-fry for 1 to 2 minutes. Add the can of tomatoes, pouring with one hand and crushing the tomatoes with the other before they hit the pan.

Cook them for around 10 minutes, stirring occasionally, then add the turmeric, chili powder, ground coriander, ground cumin, sugar, and salt. Stir, then add the potatoes and ½ cup of warm water.

Cover and cook on a medium heat for around 12 to 15 minutes, stirring, or until the potatoes are cooked (spear them with a knife to check: the potato should slide off easily). Taste and adjust the salt, sugar, and chili powder as necessary.

Serve with rice, chapatis (see page 196), or paratha (see page 198), and a sprinkling of cilantro.

CHAPATI WRAPS WITH SPICY VEGETABLES

Shaak bhareli rotli

No matter where you're from, wrapping something up in bread is a simple pleasure. India is no different. This wrap is a delight of spicy mixed vegetables and big hunks of paneer, all bundled into a chapati with a big spoonful of mint chutney.

SERVES 4 (1 WRAP EACH)

3 tablespoons canola oil

1 block of paneer (8 ounces), cut into
  ¼ x 2½-inch strips

1 large onion, finely sliced

3 cloves of garlic, finely sliced

1-inch piece of ginger, peeled and grated

1 red pepper, cut into long, thin strips

2 carrots, cut into long, thin strips

1 zucchini, cut into long, thin strips

1 tablespoon tomato paste

½ teaspoon garam masala

¾ teaspoon chili powder

1½ teaspoons ground coriander

1 teaspoon ground cumin

1¼ teaspoons salt

To serve

mint and yogurt chutney (see page 219)

4 big chapatis (see page 196, or you could use
  tortilla wraps)

1 lemon, cut into wedges

a big handful of cilantro (1½ ounces), chopped

Put a tablespoon of the oil into a large, lidded frying pan on a high heat and fry the strips of paneer. They might spit; if they do, make sure to defend yourself with a lid or half cover the pan. Fry for around 5 minutes, turning every minute, until they turn a nice golden brown on each side, then remove and set aside on a paper towel.

Put another 2 tablespoons of oil into the pan and fry the onion on a medium heat for 6 to 8 minutes, until soft and turning gold, then add the garlic and ginger. Stir, cook for a minute, then add the pepper and carrot. Cook for 10 minutes, then add the zucchini along with the tomato paste, garam masala, chili powder, coriander, cumin, and salt.

Cook for another 10 minutes with the lid on, adding a splash of water if necessary so that nothing sticks to the bottom of the pan. While the vegetables are cooking, make the mint and yogurt chutney. When the vegetables are cooked, throw the paneer back into the pan and mix. Taste the mixture, adjusting the seasoning as required.

To put the wraps together, heat the chapatis in a dry frying pan for a minute each, or until they are hot, and move to a plate. Put a quarter of the mixture down the middle of each chapati. Add a generous spoonful of chutney, a squeeze of lemon, and a scattering of cilantro. Roll up and polish off.

CAULIFLOWER, CASHEW, PEA, AND COCONUT CURRY

Phool kobi kaju anna mattar nu shaak

I ate a variation of this recipe in a small cliff-top café in Varkala, Kerala. Coconuts grow feverishly along the coastline there, and as a result end up in many South Indian dishes.

The cauliflower becomes deliciously soft and tender when cooked in coconut milk and tastes great with fresh, sweet green peas and crunchy cashews. It's substantial enough to eat on its own with just a bit of rice, and speedy enough to make midweek.

SERVES 4

1¾-inch piece of ginger, peeled and roughly chopped

4 cloves of garlic, roughly chopped

1 fresh green chili, roughly chopped (seeded if you prefer less heat)

salt

4 tablespoons canola oil

2 large onions, finely chopped

1 tablespoon tomato paste

1½ teaspoons ground coriander

1¼ teaspoons ground cumin

½ teaspoon chili powder

1 large head of cauliflower (around 1¼ pounds), broken into bite-size florets

1½ cups coconut milk

4 ounces unsalted cashews

½ cup plus 2 tablespoons garden peas, fresh or frozen

½ teaspoon garam masala

a small bunch of cilantro (½ ounce), leaves chopped

a wedge of lemon

Put the ginger, garlic, and green chili into a mortar and pestle with a pinch of salt, bash everything to a paste, and set aside.

Put 3 tablespoons of oil into a wide-bottomed, lidded frying pan on a medium heat and, when it's hot, add the onions. Fry them for 10 to 12 minutes, until golden and just turning brown, then add the ginger, garlic, and chili paste, and stir-fry for 3 to 4 minutes. Next add the tomato paste, ground coriander, cumin, chili powder, and 1¼ teaspoons of salt, then stir to mix.

Add the cauliflower florets to the pan, coat in the spices, then pour in the coconut milk. Bring to a simmer before putting the lid on, turn the heat down to low, and leave to cook for 10 to 12 minutes.

While the cauliflower is cooking, heat a tablespoon of oil in a small frying pan on a medium heat. When it's hot, fry the cashews for a minute on each side and tip on to a plate to cool.

When the cauliflower is tender, add the peas and garam masala, stir, then cook for 4 to 5 minutes. Check the seasoning, then sprinkle the cashews, cilantro, and a squeeze of lemon over the top of the curry, just before serving.

Serve with a big steaming bowl of basmati rice.

DISHA'S PAV BHAJI

I have to try hard to contain my excitement when someone gives me a recipe for something I've just eaten and fallen in love with. This is my cousin Disha's recipe for pav bhaji, which is a famous and much-loved street food in Mumbai. It's a mash of spicy vegetables slathered in butter, best mopped up with a hot "pav" – a bread roll – while the juices escape down your chin.

SERVES 4

7 ounces mashing potatoes (Yukon Gold, red or white all-purpose)

3 tablespoons unsalted butter (plus extra to finish)

2 large onions, chopped

4 cloves of garlic, crushed

1¾-inch piece of ginger, peeled and grated

2 medium eggplants (1 pound in total), cut into ¼-inch cubes

14 ounces strained tomatoes (such as Pomì)

1 tablespoon tomato paste

2 teaspoons ground cumin

2 teaspoons ground coriander

1 teaspoon garam masala

¼ teaspoon ground turmeric

optional: ½ teaspoon amchur (dried mango powder)

1½ teaspoons salt

¾ teaspoon chili powder

½ head of cauliflower (around 9 ounces), broken into ¾-inch cubes

To serve

8 to 12 soft white bread rolls

butter

1 red onion, finely chopped

a handful of cilantro

a couple of lemon wedges, to squeeze over

Peel and chop the potatoes into equal-size chunks, then boil them for around 10 minutes, or until tender. Drain, mash, then set to one side.

Put the butter into a wide-bottomed, lidded frying pan on a medium heat. When it starts to foam, add the onions and cook for 8 to 10 minutes, until golden. Add the garlic and ginger, and stir well. After a minute, add the eggplants to the pan and cover. Stir them every now and then until they're soft – this should take around 10 minutes. Add the strained tomatoes and tomato paste, and cook for around 5 to 7 minutes until it is a thick mash, rich and dark red.

Add the cumin, coriander, garam masala, and turmeric, the amchur if using, and the salt. Stir and taste, adding the chili powder if you'd like more heat. Finally, add the mashed potato and cauliflower. Stir to mix and put the lid on, leaving it to cook for around 10 minutes, or until soft.

Taste and adjust any seasoning. Transfer to a bowl and use a potato masher or a fork to mash it. The consistency should be somewhere between mashed potato and thick pasta sauce – you can add some hot water to loosen the bhaji if need be. For a final flourish, add a generous pat of butter and stir it in.

Serve with halved and toasted bread rolls, generously spread with butter. Put a layer of pav bhaji in the middle of each roll, and top with a sprinkling of red onion, cilantro, and a squeeze of lemon juice.

FRESH SPINACH AND PANEER
Palak paneer

My grandfather was an eccentric man. He wore polished patent shoes, a sharply cut suit, and smelled of jasmine behind his ears. The week he retired, he signed up for a three-month round-the-world cruise to celebrate. Before he left, he had a courtesy call from the Kitchen Head of the ship to see whether he had any dietary requirements. "I really like Indian vegetable curries," he said, and sent over a whole shipping container of Indian greens to travel with him until his return.

Spinach and paneer was one of his favorites. This is a much fresher version of the old curry-house stalwart saag paneer. I like to eat it when the spinach has only just wilted so that it still tastes fresh and keeps its goodness.

SERVES 4

canola oil

1 pound paneer, cut into ¾-inch cubes

salt

2 medium onions, finely chopped

1-inch piece of ginger, peeled, then grated or finely chopped

5 cloves of garlic, crushed

1 fresh green chili, very finely chopped

14 ounces cherry tomatoes, halved

1 tablespoon tomato paste

1½ teaspoons ground coriander

1½ teaspoons ground cumin

½ teaspoon ground turmeric

½ teaspoon chili powder

1 pound fresh spinach leaves, washed

Put 3 tablespoons of the oil into a lidded frying pan on a high heat. Lightly season the paneer cubes with salt and fry them in the pan, turning regularly until golden on each side. Watch out, as the paneer might spit; if it does, half cover it with a lid. Remove the paneer cubes using a slotted spoon and put them to one side on a paper towel.

Turn the heat down to medium, put a little more oil into the pan if need be, and add the onions. Fry for 8 to 10 minutes, until they are golden. Add the ginger, garlic, and green chili, stir well, then add the cherry tomatoes and tomato paste.

Put the lid on the pan and cook the tomatoes for 6 to 8 minutes, until they start to break down and become soft. Then add the coriander, cumin, turmeric, chili powder, and 1¼ teaspoons of salt or to taste. Stir well and taste, adding the extra chili powder if you'd like to. The mixture should look quite paste-like now and there should be very little (if any) liquid running from it. (If this is not the case, put the lid back on and cook for another 5 minutes.)

Return the paneer pieces to the pan, stir to coat them with the paste, and heat through. Finally, add the spinach in batches, wilting down a large handful before adding another, and coating the leaves carefully with the sauce.

Cook for a further 5 minutes with the lid on, to make sure all the spinach has wilted, then take off the heat. Serve with some lovely hot chapatis (see page 196) or naan (see page 199).

MATOKE
Spiced plantains with tomatoes and cilantro

When my mum's family fled Uganda for England by order of Idi Amin, they left almost everything behind, bringing with them just one suitcase (between a family of five), £50, and this recipe for matoke.

"Matoke" means "green bananas" in Swahili but is now the name of a dish created by Gujaratis who came to East Africa from India and started cooking with local ingredients. It's a rich spiced mash which is silken and creamy in texture and incredibly soothing. It's East Africa meets India on a plate.

SERVES 4

8 unripe plantains (available from most Asian and African grocers)

3 tablespoons canola oil

½ teaspoon cumin seeds

12 black peppercorns

1 large onion, finely chopped

1¾-inch piece of ginger, peeled and grated

4 cloves of garlic, crushed

1 fresh green chili, very finely chopped

3 large ripe tomatoes, roughly chopped

1 tablespoon tomato paste

⅓ teaspoon ground turmeric

½ teaspoon chili powder

¾ teaspoon salt

a really big bunch of cilantro (3 ounces), chopped

Put the plantains, skin on, in a large pan, cover with cold water, and bring to a boil on a medium heat. Boil them for around 10 minutes, until they're nice and tender and you can easily run a knife through them. Drain them, reserving some of the liquid, and put them to one side.

Put the oil into a wide-bottomed, lidded frying pan on a medium heat. When it's hot, add the cumin seeds and peppercorns and fry them for around 30 seconds, until you can smell them. Add the onion and fry over a medium heat for 8 to 10 minutes, until golden, then add the ginger, garlic, and green chili. Stir-fry for a couple of minutes, then add the tomatoes and tomato paste. Pop the lid on for 5 minutes or so, until the tomatoes start to break down and mix together. Then add the turmeric, chili powder, and salt.

Chop the plantains (skin on) into 1¾-inch chunks, then peel the skin and discard. Add the plantains to the pan, put the lid back on, and cook for a further 5 minutes. Mash the matoke pieces with a wooden spoon, adding some of the reserved water (if need be) to get a lovely creamy consistency.

Taste and adjust the salt or spices if necessary, then add the chopped cilantro and stir in.

Serve with hot chapatis (see page 196) and a generous dollop of homemade or Greek yogurt.

PAN-FRIED OKRA WITH CARAMELIZED ONIONS AND YOGURT SAUCE
Bhinda nu shaak

Gujaratis love okra, especially in a yogurt and chickpea sauce which we call "kadhi." It sets a Gujarati heart a-flutter. Okra can turn gloopy when cooking though, because the seeds don't like moisture very much. I've found the best way to deal with this is to fry the okra on a high heat and in small batches, so that they crisp up nicely. You can then toss them with the onions and cover with the sauce just before serving.

SERVES 4

1-inch piece of ginger, peeled and roughly chopped
6 cloves of garlic, roughly chopped
salt
5 tablespoons canola oil
1 teaspoon mustard seeds
2 large red onions, thinly sliced
¾ teaspoon chili powder
1 teaspoon ground cumin

1½ pounds okra, trimmed and halved
  lengthways

For the hot yogurt sauce
¾ cup whole-milk yogurt
1 tablespoon chickpea flour (besan)
¼ teaspoon ground turmeric
1 teaspoon salt

Put the ginger and garlic into a mortar and pestle along with a pinch of salt, and bash to a coarse paste.

Pour 3 tablespoons of oil into a large frying pan on a medium heat and, when it's hot, add the mustard seeds. When the seeds pop, add the red onions. When they are soft and tender, add the ginger and garlic paste, chili powder, and cumin. Carry on cooking the onions, stirring occasionally, for around 15 minutes or until they are caramelized, then tip them into a large mixing bowl.

Wipe the pan clean if need be, put 2 tablespoons of oil into it, on a high heat, and when the pan is really hot, throw in the okra, being careful not to crowd the pan and making sure that each okra is touching the bottom of the pan.

Season with salt and fry for around 4 to 5 minutes until they are nicely browned, only moving them around every minute or so. When the okra are crispy on the outside but soft to the touch, remove them from the pan and put to one side. Then repeat in small batches.

To make the sauce, put the yogurt, chickpea flour, turmeric, and salt into a pan, mix together and heat until warm but not bubbling. Take off the heat. Carefully fold together the onions and the okra in the bowl. Serve on one large plate, or divide between four plates, and spoon over the yogurt sauce. Eat with chapatis (see page 196) or paratha (see page 198).

ROASTED ALOO GOBI SALAD

Phool kobi ne bateta nu salaad

You're probably on first-name terms with aloo gobi, although you won't recognize this dish. It uses the same companions – potato and cauliflower – but gives them a well-earned makeover. Here they are roasted until crisp and served with papadums, wilted spinach, and chickpeas, with some mint chutney thrown in for good measure. The key to making this salad is to get everything ready so you can throw it all together at the last minute, just before serving.

SERVES 4

4 papadums (either cooked or uncooked)

mint and yogurt chutney (see page 219)

14 ounces new potatoes

1¼ pounds cauliflower (2 small heads or 1 large)

1 teaspoon cumin seeds, crushed

3 cloves of garlic, crushed

1 teaspoon chili flakes

salt

ground black pepper

6 tablespoons canola oil

2 medium red onions, finely sliced

1 14-ounce can of black chickpeas (kala chana), although white will do

1 pound spinach leaves

4 ounces red-skinned (or unsalted) peanuts

lemon wedges, to serve

Preheat the oven to 350°F.

I like to serve this salad in papadum bowls. If you're making your own, follow the instructions on page 270, but equally you could serve them on the side.

Whip up the mint and yogurt chutney. Chop the new potatoes into ¾-inch cubes, and break or chop the cauliflower into small florets, just bigger than the potatoes. Keep the potatoes and cauliflower separate and pop them in a single layer onto two baking trays.

Distribute the cumin seeds, garlic, and chili flakes over the vegetables, and season generously with salt and a few grinds of the pepper mill. Drizzle the vegetables with 4 tablespoons of oil and mix it in with your hands so that they are well coated. Put the cauliflower and potatoes in the oven for 25 to 30 minutes, turning halfway through so the potatoes don't stick. When done and just starting to brown, remove and set aside.

Meanwhile put 2 tablespoons of oil into a frying pan on a medium heat. Add the onions and fry, stirring occasionally, until they are caramelized; this will take around 15 minutes. When the onions are done, add the chickpeas, stir for a couple of minutes, then add the spinach and cook until just wilted.

Mix in the potatoes and cauliflower and check for seasoning, then distribute across the papadum bowls or plates. Drizzle some mint and yogurt chutney dressing over the top and scatter over the peanuts to finish. Serve with wedges of lemon.

SLOW-COOKED RED PEPPER AND PANEER CURRY

Karahi paneer

This is a simple way to turn a bunch of peppers into the star of the show. It's a great dish to cook when you're feeling lazy, as the longer you leave peppers to cook, the better they taste.

While eating paneer with peppers is commonplace in India, traditionally they're cooked quickly – but I like my peppers slow-cooked so that they develop a sweet, smoky flavor, which perfectly complements creamy fresh paneer.

SERVES 4

1½ teaspoons cumin seeds

1 tablespoon coriander seeds

4 tablespoons canola oil

2 medium onions, thinly sliced

4 fat cloves of garlic, crushed

1-inch piece of ginger, peeled and grated

1 fresh green chili, very finely chopped

4 red peppers (1 pound), cut into ⅛-inch strips

6 tomatoes, roughly chopped

½ teaspoon ground turmeric

¼ teaspoon chili powder

1¼ teaspoons salt

1 pound paneer, cut into ¾-inch cubes

a handful of chopped cilantro, to serve

In a large saucepan, dry-roast the cumin and coriander seeds over a high heat for a couple of minutes, stirring frequently until the coriander seeds are a pale gold color. Tip them out into a mortar and pestle, crush them into a powder and set aside.

Put 3 tablespoons of oil into the same pan on a high heat and, when it's hot, add the onions. Stir-fry for around 5 minutes, until translucent, then add the garlic, ginger, green chili, and peppers. Cook for another 5 minutes, stirring frequently, until the peppers start to break down, then add the tomatoes, the coriander and cumin powder, the turmeric, chili powder, and salt.

Turn the heat down to low to medium and continue to cook for around 30 minutes, stirring every now and then. Do keep checking it from time to time to ensure it's not burning and add water if you need to loosen the mixture.

Meanwhile, heat a tablespoon of oil in another frying pan on a high heat and, when it's hot, add the cubes of paneer. Be careful as they might spit; if they do, half cover the pan with a lid. Fry the cubes until they are an appetizing golden color on each side, then remove them from the pan and put to one side.

When the peppers are cooked through (soft enough to cut with a wooden spoon), add the paneer, mix everything together, and taste for seasoning, adjusting it if need be.

Serve with the cilantro stirred through, my golden garlic raita (see page 178), and some naan (see page 199).

TOMATO FRY
Tamatar nu shaak

You say "tomato," Gujaratis say "tamatar"; either way, it is definitely one of my desert island top-five ingredients. In Indian cooking, tomatoes usually play a supporting role and rarely get a chance to shine, but this curry really champions them.

The secret is to use the best and ripest tomatoes you can find. You'll know when you've found them as they'll smell warm and excited, like they've spent too much time in the sunshine. Sometimes we will throw in a couple of handfuls of sev (chickpea noodles; see page 308) right at the end, which is definitely worth trying if you have some.

SERVES 4

3 tablespoons canola oil
1 teaspoon mustard seeds
optional: 20 fresh curry leaves
2 large red onions, finely sliced
2-inch piece of ginger, peeled and finely grated
6 cloves of garlic, crushed
2 pounds 2 ounces ripe medium tomatoes, cut into ¾-inch wedges

1½ teaspoons ground cumin
1½ teaspoons ground coriander
½ teaspoon ground turmeric
1 teaspoon ground black pepper
¾ teaspoon chili powder
1¼ teaspoons salt

Put the oil into a large frying pan on a medium heat and, when it's hot, add the mustard seeds and, if using, the curry leaves. When the mustard seeds start to pop, add the onions, ginger, and garlic and fry them, stirring frequently, for 8 to 10 minutes, until the onions are soft and turning a golden-brown color.

Add the tomatoes and fry them for around 10 minutes, stirring occasionally. Add the ground cumin, coriander, turmeric, black pepper, chili powder, and salt, and stir. Cook for a further minute or two, then take off the heat. The sauce should be brick red and thick. Taste and adjust any seasoning.

Serve with some fresh hot naan (see page 199) to mop up the tomatoey juices.

SAUTÉED SPRING VEGETABLES WITH SPICES

Come springtime, Lincolnshire is bursting at the seams with beans, scallions, and asparagus. More often than not, we'll come home with bagfuls of them, very lightly spice whatever we have to make the most of them, and eat them with some bread or a steaming bowl of basmati rice.

SERVES 2

3 tablespoons canola oil

1 teaspoon mustard seeds

1 large onion, finely chopped

4 cloves of garlic, crushed

3 large leeks, very finely cut into rings

8–9 ounces mixed spring vegetables, such as green beans and snow peas, chopped into 1-inch pieces

9 ounces asparagus, chopped into 1-inch pieces

½ teaspoon ground turmeric

½ teaspoon chili powder

½ teaspoon ground coriander

¾ teaspoon salt

2 handfuls of peas (frozen are fine)

lemon wedges, to garnish

Put a pan of water on to boil, as you'll need this later to blanch the beans and asparagus.

Put the oil into a wide-bottomed, lidded frying pan on a medium heat and, when it's hot, add the mustard seeds. Wait for them to pop, then add the onion. Fry the onion for 6 to 8 minutes, until translucent and soft but not brown, then add the garlic and leeks.

Meanwhile, throw the beans and asparagus into the pan of boiling water for 2 to 3 minutes to blanch them. Stir the leeks occasionally and keep cooking them until they are soft and lose their shape. Then add the turmeric, chili powder, coriander, and salt and stir to mix.

Drain the blanched veg and add to the pan along with the peas, leave them to cook for a couple of minutes, then take off the heat.

Serve with a squeeze of lemon, some rice, or some buttered chapatis (see page 196).

SIMPLY SPICED
SPRING CABBAGE
Kobi nu shaak

When you look at this dish you will probably think it is too simple to be exciting or substantial, but it is a delicious combination, especially when eaten with chapatis, yogurt, and perhaps a bit of "attanu," or pickle.

It is very quick to make and can be eaten with other dishes, perhaps a dal (see page 166) or as part of a bigger feast with lamb raan (see page 114). For a bit of variation, try adding small cubes of potatoes to the pan after frying the onion and before adding the cabbage, or a handful of freshly grated coconut just before serving.

SERVES 2 AS A MAIN DISH OR 4 AS A SIDE

2 tablespoons canola oil

2 teaspoons mustard seeds

1 large onion, finely sliced

1 white cabbage (around 1½ pounds), finely shredded

½ teaspoon ground turmeric

1 teaspoon salt

1 teaspoon ground cumin

¾ teaspoon chili powder

1 tablespoon tomato paste

Put the oil into a wide-bottomed, lidded frying pan on a medium heat and, when it's hot, add the mustard seeds. When they start to pop, add the onion and fry for around 6 to 8 minutes, until it is nice and soft.

Add the shredded cabbage and ¼ cup of warm water, stir, and pop the lid on. Allow to cook through for 5 minutes, then add the turmeric, salt, cumin, chili powder, and tomato paste. Stir, pop the lid on again, and cook for another 6 to 8 minutes, until the cabbage is really soft without any crunch left in it.

Serve with chapatis (see page 196) and a dollop of yogurt on the side.

SPROUTED BEANS WITH GARLIC, LEMON, AND CUMIN

Funguyela mug nu shaak

This is a very popular Gujarati dish, and everyone in the family loves it in the summertime. We sprout our own beans and watch as these hard, dry pantry staples transform into fresh, crisp sprouts. They make for a crunchy and tangy stir-fry when seasoned with browned garlic, lemon, and cumin – flavors that Gujaratis absolutely love.

The health benefits of sprouted beans have long been touted by nutritionists, as they're packed full of protein, B vitamins, vitamin C, and iron. It's also a great way to get the most out of your mung beans without having to boil them. For how to grow your own sprouts, see page 271; alternatively, you might be able to get them in your local supermarket or Indian grocer's shop.

SERVES 4 AS PART OF A WIDER SPREAD (WITH ANOTHER MAIN DISH AND SOME RICE OR BREAD)

2 tablespoons canola oil

½ teaspoon cumin seeds

4 cloves of garlic, finely sliced

1¼ pounds sprouted beans (made from 7–8 ounces dry beans)

1 heaped teaspoon tomato paste

1¼ teaspoons salt

1 teaspoon sugar

½ teaspoon ground turmeric

½ teaspoon chili powder

juice of ½ lemon

a small bunch of cilantro (½ ounce), leaves finely chopped

Put the oil into a wide-bottomed, lidded frying pan on a medium heat and, when it's hot, add the cumin seeds. After 30 seconds or so, add the sliced garlic, and when the garlic turns light brown add the sprouted beans. Pour in ½ cup of warm water, cover with the lid, and leave to cook through for around 5 minutes.

Add the tomato paste, salt, sugar, turmeric, and chili powder, stir them through to mix, and put the lid back on for another minute. Before serving, give it a good squeeze of lemon and stir the cilantro leaves through.

Serve hot or cold, in bowls, with some yogurt and chapatis (see page 196) on the side.

MEAT

03

MEAT

In India, religion has shaped which animals are eaten and which are allowed to wander down the streets. Indian Muslims don't eat pigs, Hindus don't eat beef, and neither eat lamb because of a bias towards goat meat (which is confusingly called mutton). This means that cows and the occasional wild boar roam free, making a wonderful nuisance of themselves by sleeping in the middle of the road or wandering into shops before being shooed out by the owners.

Here in England my family stays true to the Indian way, in that we don't eat beef. Instead, when it comes to meat, we tend to go for lamb, goat, chicken, and any other interesting local birds we can get our hands on, such as quail or pheasant.

In fact, until my grandfather Mathuradas Lakhani came on to the scene, our immediate ancestors were vegetarian. While he grew up in a modest family in a small village, Ranakandora, he had a voracious appetite for life and adventure and wanted to try everything, including meat. He traveled widely, eating pork, goat, lamb, fish, shellfish, and even antelope, and bringing various recipes and animals back into the family kitchen. If there is anyone to thank for the fact that this isn't a vegetarian cookbook, it's him.

The recipes in this chapter originate from all across India – some collected by my grandfather, some by my mother and some by me – and the odd Ugandan dish, such as the Ugandan quail poacher's stew (see page 102), has slipped in there, too.

Whatever the meat, most curries were traditionally cooked on a stove, and kebabs or grilled meat on a "sagdi," or open wood fire. Ovens didn't really exist, although on the odd occasion my grandfather would create his own by digging a hole in the ground, starting a small fire and baking an antelope wrapped in banana leaves overnight, until the meat fell apart.

The bones are traditionally left in the meat, because the marrow in them contributes to the silkiness and flavor of a sauce. The best way to eat these is with your hands, noisily sucking the bone marrow out at the table.

Nowadays I'm lucky enough to have a farmers' market on my doorstep, and I buy my meat there. For a lamb or goat curry I like to use shoulder or the thriftier neck: both cuts are robust and can take a lot of spice, and fall apart beautifully when slow-cooked, becoming soft and sticky. Shoulder is great for cooking lamb kebabs quickly, too, as it's such a moist cut that it tastes tender after just a few minutes on a barbecue or in a grill pan.

On the subject of chickens, it really is true that compromising on welfare isn't just a bad idea in its own right but also means you're compromising on taste. I tend to go for thighs and legs over breast meat as they're much more tender and succulent (and they're also a lot cheaper).

WHOLE ROAST
MASALA CHICKEN _Masala murghi_

Love has been compared to the scent of roses, but I think the smell of a roast chicken is much more romantic. I am crazy about this chicken dish, which came to my kitchen via my friend Raoul and really is the best of both worlds: the classic Western roast chicken and some of the best flavors India has to offer. The toasted sweet spices dance around the almonds and make it a real treat to eat. It's also fantastic for leftovers, if there are any.

As with all marinades, this one works best when left alone to do its thing for a decent length of time. I marinate the chicken for at least an hour, but you can marinate it for up to 12 hours for maximum flavor.

SERVES 4

1 tablespoon cumin seeds

¾ tablespoon coriander seeds

2-inch cinnamon stick

5 cloves

1 teaspoon black peppercorns

¼ cup ground almonds

¼ teaspoon ground turmeric

4 tablespoons whole-milk yogurt

1¾ level teaspoons salt

¼ medium onion, roughly chopped

3 cloves of garlic, roughly chopped

1 large chicken (around 3½ pounds)

Put the cumin seeds and coriander seeds into a dry frying pan over a high heat until the coriander seeds turn from meadow green to a lightly toasted golden color. Tip the toasted spices into a mortar and pestle or a spice grinder, along with the cinnamon stick, cloves, and peppercorns, and grind together. Put them into a big bowl and add the ground almonds, turmeric, yogurt, and salt.

Bash the onion and garlic to a pulp with a small pinch of salt, then add this to the bowl and mix thoroughly.

Get an oven dish big enough to hold the chicken in, and line the dish with foil. Make a small slit at the bottom of the chicken breast on both sides, then rub some of the spice marinade between the skin and flesh, getting into the nooks and crannies. Don't be shy now. Rub the rest of the marinade all over the chicken. Cover with foil and leave in the fridge to marinate for at least 1 hour and up to 12 hours.

When you're ready to cook the chicken, preheat the oven to 400°F.

When the oven is hot, cover the chicken loosely with foil (so that the marinade does not burn) and cook for 1 hour. Remove the foil after an hour and cook for another 20 minutes to brown it nicely on top. Check that the chicken is done by piercing a thigh with a knife and making sure that the juices run clear.

Serve with my ferrari potatoes (see page 177) and spinach with black pepper, garlic, and lemon (see page 179).

CREAMY CHICKEN AND FIG CURRY *Anjeer murghi*

This is a pot of deliciousness: a mildly spiced, warming curry with a delicate sweet flavor. It's made with dried fruit and yogurt, and if you're a fan of chicken korma, you will love this. Despite its decadence, it is a simple curry to cook and can be made predominantly with pantry ingredients, so it's an easy dish for last-minute guests or a midweek dinner. I make it over and over again, because for very little time and effort you get something really gorgeous.

Because it's a rich dish, it's best served with something green, such as my green beans with mustard seeds and ginger (see page 181), or spinach with black pepper, garlic, and lemon (see page 179).

SERVES 4

10 soft dried figs

1¾ pounds skinless, boneless chicken thighs

1 cup plus 2 tablespoons homemade or Greek yogurt

1 teaspoon garam masala

1¼ teaspoons salt

¾ teaspoon chili powder

2 tablespoons canola oil

1½ large (or 2 small) white onions, finely sliced

1 cinnamon stick

4 cloves of garlic, crushed

1¾-inch piece of ginger, peeled and finely grated

Boil the kettle and pour boiling water over the dried figs in a heatproof bowl to soften them. Leave them to soak while you deal with the rest of the ingredients.

Pick over the chicken thighs to remove any fat, then chop them into ¾ x 1-inch pieces. Put them into a large bowl, along with the yogurt, garam masala, salt, and chili powder. Drain the figs and chop them into ¼-inch cubes. Add them to the chicken mixture, stir until well mixed, and set aside.

Put the oil into a wide-bottomed, lidded frying pan on a medium heat and, when it's hot, add the onions and the cinnamon stick. Fry over a medium heat until they are soft and golden.

Add the garlic and ginger and cook through for 4 to 5 minutes before adding the chicken mixture. Put the lid on the pan and leave to cook for 15 to 20 minutes, stirring every 5 minutes or so. The color of the curry will darken as it cooks, and the liquid will start to reduce, creating a lovely thick sauce.

Remember to take out the cinnamon stick, and serve with a big bowl of basmati rice (or bread if you prefer) and some greens.

PISTACHIO AND YOGURT CHICKEN CURRY
Pista nu murghi

This rich and mildly spiced dish is fit for a maharajah. In fact the inspiration for this dish came from a book I picked up on my travels in India: *Cooking Delights of the Maharajahs*, written by a former prince of Sailana, Digvijaya Singh. He loved the exotic Mughlai dishes served up in his kitchens so much that he learned and recorded every single one.

The ground pistachios lend themselves perfectly to the sweetness of the onions and create a beautiful, rich, creamy sauce. You'll need a spice grinder, ideally, or food processor to grind the nuts for this recipe.

SERVES 4

4 ounces unsalted pistachios (plus extra to serve)

2-inch piece of ginger, peeled and roughly chopped

4 cloves of garlic, roughly chopped

3 tablespoons canola oil

2 large onions, sliced into fine rings

2 large ripe tomatoes, roughly chopped

¼ teaspoon ground black pepper

1 teaspoon garam masala

½ teaspoon chili powder

1 tablespoon coriander seeds, crushed

½ teaspoon ground cardamom

1¾-inch cinnamon stick or 1 teaspoon ground cinnamon

1 teaspoon salt (or to taste)

1¾ pounds skinless, boneless chicken thighs, chopped into ¾-inch cubes

1 cup hot chicken stock

4 tablespoons homemade or Greek yogurt (plus extra to serve)

juice of ½ lemon

In a food processor or spice grinder, grind the pistachios to a fine powder and set aside. Bash up the ginger and garlic in a mortar and pestle to a coarse paste and set aside.

Put the oil in a wide-bottomed, lidded frying pan on a medium heat and, when it's hot, add the onions. Fry until caramelized, which should take around 20 minutes. Add the garlic and ginger paste and stir-fry for 3 to 4 minutes before adding the tomatoes.

Put the lid on the pan and let the tomatoes cook for around 5 minutes, until they start to break down, then add the black pepper, garam masala, chili powder, coriander, cardamom, cinnamon, and salt. Stir, then add the chicken pieces to the pan.

Turn the chicken so that it seals on all sides, then add the ground pistachios. Stir-fry for a minute, then pour in the chicken stock. Lightly whisk the yogurt with a fork, then stir it into the pan. Pop the lid on the pan and leave to cook for around 15 minutes. Taste the dish and adjust as you wish. Add a little water to get a good saucy consistency if need be. To serve, spoon over a dollop of yogurt, scatter with chopped pistachios, and squeeze over the lemon juice. Eat with a bowl of basmati rice or some naan (see page 199).

GARLIC CHICKEN CHAAT

Lasan anna murghi nu chaat

This delightful textured salad of pan-fried garlicky chicken legs, crunchy papadums, and fresh vegetables makes for a great summer's night dinner. Chutney is a happy accompaniment – the mint and yogurt chutney (see page 219) or sweet and hot tomato chutney (see page 218) in particular.

SERVES 4

For the garlic chicken

2 tablespoons canola oil

2 tablespoons unsalted butter

4 chicken legs (around 2 pounds 2 ounces in total)

salt

ground black pepper

6 cloves of garlic

½ teaspoon chili flakes

For the salad

½ cucumber (around 10 ounces)

9 ounces ripe baby plum tomatoes, quartered

1 small red onion

1 fresh green chili (or ½ if you prefer less heat), seeded

a big bunch of cilantro (1½ ounces)

1 14-ounce can of black chickpeas (kala chana), rinsed and drained (although white will do)

juice of ½ lime

1 tablespoon canola oil

⅓ teaspoon salt

½ teaspoon chaat masala (see page 287)

1½ teaspoons sugar

4 papadums, to serve

First make the garlic chicken. Put the oil into a wide-bottomed, lidded frying pan on a medium-high heat, then add the butter. When the butter starts to foam, add the chicken legs. Season with salt and pepper and fry until they are a nice golden color, which should take around 5 minutes, turning them over to brown both sides. Smash the garlic cloves a little with the back of a knife and add them to the pan along with the chili flakes, and when the chicken legs have an appetizing color, turn the heat to low and pop the lid on the pan. Leave to cook for 30 minutes, turning the legs halfway through.

Meanwhile, cut the cucumber in half lengthways, scoop out the seeds, chop it into ¾-inch chunks, and put into a large bowl. Chop the baby tomatoes to the same size and add them to the bowl. Dice the red onion as finely as you can, slice the green chili and cilantro leaves very finely, and throw these into the bowl too, along with the black chickpeas. Make the dressing by combining the lime juice, oil, salt, chaat masala powder, and sugar in a small jam jar. Pop the lid on the jar, give it a good shake and pour over the salad.

Next cook the papadums (see page 270), or if already cooked, leave to one side.

When the chicken is done, take it off the heat. Put a quarter of the salad on each plate, lay each leg on the side, and spoon over some of the chutney you're serving it with. Serve with papadums on the side.

ROASTED TAMARIND CHICKEN WITH HONEY AND RED CHILI

Ambli anna mudh wari murghi

While it's not common to use honey in Indian cooking, my "uncle" Raymond, our neighbor in Lincolnshire, was a beekeeper, so we grew up with cupboards full of the stuff and it's found its way into my cooking. I like the way it balances out the sharp taste of the tamarind and the heat of the chili to form a glaze for the chicken, which browns beautifully when roasted.

I usually serve this chicken with chapatis (see page 196), my kachumbar (see page 185), and my mint and yogurt chutney (see page 219).

SERVES 2 (BUT YOU CAN EASILY DOUBLE THIS RECIPE)

14 ounces bone-in chicken thighs

½ teaspoon chili powder

1 teaspoon salt (or to taste)

½ teaspoon ground black pepper

1½ teaspoons tamarind paste

2 cloves of garlic, crushed

3 tablespoons honey

Preheat your oven to 350°F. Line an oven tray big enough to accommodate the chicken thighs comfortably with foil.

In a large mixing bowl, mix together the chili powder, salt, black pepper, tamarind paste, garlic, and honey. Add the chicken to the bowl and use your hands to mix everything together well.

Transfer the chicken to the roasting tray and roast for 20 to 25 minutes in the hot oven until the chicken skin is a crispy golden brown.

COCONUT AND TAMARIND CHICKEN CURRY

Nariyal anna ambli waru murghi

Coconut and tamarind is a famous pairing in South Indian cooking. In the same way that milk will take the edge off a strong coffee, coconut milk takes the sharp edges off tamarind's sourness, creating in this dish a balanced and creamy chicken curry with a bit of a kick. Both coconut milk and tamarind paste are readily available, which makes this a quick midweek curry to whip up.

SERVES 4

2 tablespoons canola oil

1 cinnamon stick, broken in two

10 fresh curry leaves (not essential, but lovely)

1 large onion, sliced

4 cloves of garlic, crushed

1¾-inch piece of ginger, peeled and grated

1 fresh red chili, finely chopped

½ teaspoon ground turmeric

1½ teaspoons ground coriander

1 teaspoon sugar

1 teaspoon salt

1¾ pounds skinless, boneless chicken thighs, chopped into 1-inch cubes

1 teaspoon tamarind paste

1½ cups coconut milk

Put the oil into a wide-bottomed, lidded frying pan on a medium heat. Add the cinnamon stick and the curry leaves (if you're using them), and allow them to infuse into the oil. Add the onion and fry, stirring occasionally, for 8 to 10 minutes, until softer and browning at the edges.

Next put the garlic and ginger into the pan and stir-fry for a couple more minutes. Add the red chili, turmeric, coriander, sugar, and salt, stir well, then put the chicken pieces into the pan.

Sear the chicken on all sides, add the tamarind paste, stir, and pour in the coconut milk. Pop the lid on the pan and cook for 15 to 20 minutes. The curry should be a lovely golden color. Eat it quickly with some steaming basmati rice, and don't forget to take out the cinnamon stick.

CHICKEN IN PICKLING SPICES
Achari murghi

If, like me, in the dark of the night you have found yourself craving the tang, bite, heat and spice that only a pickle can satisfy (often alongside a hunk of cheese), then I imagine you will like this dish very much. It puts the same spices – nigella, fennel, mustard, and cumin seeds – which are often used in Indian chutneys and pickles to great use, resulting in a tangy and very addictive curry.

Don't be put off by the long list of ingredients; almost half are whipped from a jar into the pan with no other effort required on your part.

SERVES 4 PICKLE LOVERS

1¾-inch piece of ginger, peeled and roughly chopped

6 cloves of garlic, roughly chopped

1 fresh green chili, roughly chopped

salt

3 tablespoons canola oil

1 teaspoon nigella seeds

1 teaspoon fennel seeds

1 teaspoon mustard seeds

1 teaspoon cumin seeds

½ teaspoon fenugreek seeds

2 large onions, finely chopped

3 medium ripe tomatoes, roughly chopped

2 tablespoons tomato paste

optional: ¾ teaspoon chili powder

½ teaspoon ground turmeric

1¾ pounds skinless, boneless chicken thighs, chopped into 1¾ x 1-inch pieces

3 tablespoons homemade or Greek yogurt

1 lemon, quartered, to serve

First put the ginger, garlic, and fresh green chili into a mortar and pestle with a pinch of salt and bash it up to a fine paste. Put it to one side.

Then put the oil into a wide-bottomed, lidded frying pan on a medium heat and, when it's hot, add the nigella, fennel, mustard, cumin, and fenugreek seeds. Stir-fry, to ensure they don't burn, for around 1 minute, until the kitchen smells spicy, then add the onions and fry until soft and golden.

Put the ginger, garlic, and green chili paste into the pan, stirring to mix. After a couple of minutes, add the tomatoes, tomato paste, the chili powder (if you would like a bit of extra heat), turmeric, and 1 level teaspoon of salt (or to taste), stir well, and cook for a further 5 minutes.

Put your chicken pieces into the pan, coat in the tomato mixture and seal the chicken on all sides. Add a splash of water, turn the heat to low, and put the lid on the pan. Cook for around 20 minutes.

Now put the yogurt into a bowl, add a few tablespoons of the chicken curry sauce, whisk with a fork, and put it into the pan, stirring it in thoroughly. (Adding the hot sauce to the yogurt will mean it's unlikely to split when mixed into the curry.) Leave the lid off the pan and cook through for another 5 minutes to reduce the sauce, then turn off the heat.

Serve with basmati rice, in four large bowls, with a good squeeze of lemon over the top.

CILANTRO CHUTNEY
CHICKEN *Lilli chatni anna murghi kari*

Lilli chatni, or cilantro chutney (see page 212), will most likely be found on every Gujarati family's kitchen table at dinner time. I make it regularly and always keep a jar of it in the fridge. I love eating it with samosas, on bread, with cheese, or whatever else is happy to sit underneath it while I carry it into my mouth. But when there's some left over, it also makes for a magnificent curry when combined with chicken.

Although you will need to make the chutney before cooking this curry, it takes very little effort: you just need to combine a few ingredients in a blender and blitz.

SERVES 4

2-inch piece of ginger, peeled and roughly chopped

6 cloves of garlic, roughly chopped

¾ fresh green chili, roughly chopped (seeded if you prefer less heat)

salt

2 tablespoons canola oil

2 onions, finely sliced

1¾ pounds skinless, boneless chicken thighs, chopped into ¾ x 1-inch pieces

6 tablespoons cilantro chutney

Throw the ginger, garlic, and green chili into a mortar and pestle, along with a pinch of salt, and bash up to a coarse paste.

Put the oil into a wide-bottomed, lidded frying pan on a medium heat. When it's hot, add the onions and fry, stirring occasionally, for 6 to 8 minutes, until they are starting to turn golden. Transfer half of the onions to a bowl and put to one side.

Add the ginger, garlic, and green chili paste and cook for around 3 minutes. Put the chicken pieces into the pan, sear them on all sides and add the chutney. Stir the chutney, pop the lid on, and turn the heat down to medium-low. Cook for around 15 minutes until the chicken is cooked through and tender.

In the meantime, transfer the onions from the bowl into a small frying pan and continue to cook them on a medium heat for another 10 to 15 minutes, until they are dark brown, soft, and sweet, then take them off the heat.

Add ½ teaspoon of salt (or to taste) to the chicken little by little, until it tastes just right, then take it off the heat.

Scatter the caramelized onions over the top of the curry just before serving. Serve alongside some steaming hot basmati rice or a pile of hot, homemade chapatis (see page 196).

MUM'S CHICKEN CURRY

I left Lincolnshire at the age of 18 to go to university in London. Secretly homesick, I would stop in Indian-owned newsstands on the way back from class, lingering over the magazines and quietly listening to the owners speaking in Gujarati, just for comfort.

When it came to food, I was at the mercy of the dorm chef, a Jamaican with an adventurous streak who would create delights such as corn and strawberry salad, indiscriminately seasoning everything with pepper. With every bite, I'd be thinking about home and my ultimate comfort food, my mum's chicken curry.

SERVES 4

2 tablespoons ghee or unsalted butter

1 tablespoon canola oil

1 teaspoon cumin seeds

2 1¾-inch cinnamon sticks

2 large onions, finely chopped

2½-inch piece of ginger, peeled and grated

6 cloves of garlic, crushed

2 fresh green chilis (or 1 teaspoon chili powder)

salt

¾ cup plus 2 tablespoons strained tomatoes (such as Pomì)

2 tablespoons tomato paste

1½ teaspoons ground cumin

½ teaspoon ground turmeric

3 tablespoons whole-milk yogurt (plus extra to serve)

2 pounds 3 ounces skinless chicken legs, or 1¾ pounds skinless, boneless chicken thighs

3 tablespoons ground almonds

1 teaspoon garam masala

Put the ghee and oil into a wide-bottomed, lidded frying pan on a medium heat and, when it's hot, add the cumin seeds and cinnamon sticks. Let them infuse in the oil for a minute, and then add the onions. Cook for 10 to 12 minutes, stirring occasionally, until golden brown.

Meanwhile, put the ginger, garlic, and green chilis into a mortar and pestle with a pinch of salt and bash to a coarse paste.

Add the paste to the pan and cook gently for 2 minutes, then pour in the strained tomatoes and stir. Cook the strained tomatoes for a few minutes until the mixture resembles a thick paste, then add the tomato paste, ground cumin, turmeric, and ½ teaspoon of salt (or to taste).

Whisk the yogurt and add it slowly to the curry. Cook it through until it starts to bubble, then add the chicken. Pop the lid on the pan and continue to cook on a gentle heat for around 30 minutes. Add the ground almonds and the garam masala and cook for another 5 minutes.

Serve with a tower of chapatis (see page 196), hot fluffy naan (see page 199), or rice, and offer yogurt at the table.

UGANDAN QUAIL POACHER'S STEW

Quail is a distant relative of the Ugandan kanga bird, which was a dinnertime favorite in my mum's house. Kangas were so prized by the Ugandans that people would run into the reeds, around elephants, and under giraffes to catch them. Luckily, you only need to go to a local butcher or supermarket to get your quail.

This is a lovely stew and a theatrical table dish which is great for sharing. Serve on a bed of rice and encourage people to dig in with their hands.

SERVES 4

4 to 6 big quail (around 7 ounces each)
salt
ground black pepper
4 tablespoons peanut oil
5 cardamom pods
5 cloves
10 black peppercorns
2 onions, finely chopped
8 cloves of garlic, finely sliced

2 teaspoons ground cumin
2 teaspoons ground coriander
½ teaspoon chili powder
1 fresh green chili, halved
1 14-ounce can of chickpeas, rinsed and drained
2½ cups hot chicken stock
½ teaspoon garam masala

Season the quail with salt and pepper. Put 2 tablespoons of oil in a large, heavy-bottomed casserole dish on a high heat. When hot, brown the quail on both sides for around 6 to 8 minutes in total, remove, and set to one side.

Put another 2 tablespoons of oil into the casserole dish, then add the cardamom pods, cloves, and peppercorns. Stir-fry for a minute, then lower the heat to medium, and add the onions. Fry for 8 to 10 minutes, until they are soft and golden. Add the garlic and stir-fry for 2 to 3 minutes.

Put the cumin, coriander, chili powder, and green chili into the casserole dish and stir. Add the chickpeas to the dish, followed by the quail and then the stock. The stock should just cover the quail.

Bring to a boil, cover the dish, then turn the heat down to low. Simmer for around an hour, until the quail is very soft and tender. Finally, add the garam masala and season the dish with salt to taste.

My cinnamon and clove pilau with cashew nuts (see page 156) is a lovely accompaniment to this dish.

A SIMPLE GOAT AND POTATO CURRY

Bakra nu kari

Goat meat makes up the majority of meat curries in India. Many Indians don't like the taste of lamb, and goat is a much leaner meat. My grandma used to cook kid goat like this, with potatoes, before switching to using lamb because it was more widely available in Lincolnshire. Nowadays goat meat can be found fairly easily, especially from halal butchers.

Goat meat is not dissimilar to mutton in flavor, in that it is rich and tasty, but it's earthier. It's a bit tougher than mutton, so needs longer cooking, but it falls apart beautifully in a couple of hours to become sticky and soft. This particular recipe is from the family archives – it's a rustic stew that takes me back to many meals on my travels around India.

SERVES 4

1¾-inch piece of ginger, peeled and roughly chopped

4 cloves of garlic, roughly chopped

1 fresh green chili, finely chopped

salt

4 tablespoons canola oil

1 teaspoon cumin seeds

½ teaspoon black peppercorns

1 cinnamon stick

1 large onion, sliced

2 pounds goat shoulder, chopped into 1 x 1¾-inch pieces (get your butcher to do this for you)

2 teaspoons ground coriander

1 teaspoon ground cumin

½ teaspoon ground turmeric

1½ cups hot vegetable stock

¾ pound potatoes

1 teaspoon chili powder

In a mortar and pestle, bash together the ginger, garlic, and green chili with a big pinch of salt to a coarse paste.

Put the oil into a large, heavy-bottomed casserole dish on a high heat. When it's hot, add the cumin seeds, peppercorns, and cinnamon stick. Stir-fry for around a minute, then add the onion. Fry for around 5 minutes, until the onion turns translucent, at which point add the ginger, garlic, and chili paste. Stir well and continue to fry for around 10 minutes, until the onion is starting to brown.

Add the diced goat, along with the coriander, cumin, and turmeric. Stir together, pour in the stock, and bring the mixture to a boil, then turn the heat down to a simmer and put the lid on the dish. Leave to cook for an hour, checking intermittently to ensure that the goat is still moist.

Peel and chop the potatoes into 1¾-inch cubes. Add to the goat, with 1½ teaspoons of salt and the chili powder, stir well, and cover the dish again. Leave it to cook for another 30 minutes, or until the potatoes are tender and you can easily pull the meat apart. Taste, and adjust the salt and chili as you wish.

Eat with chapatis (see page 196) or rice.

WILD PHEASANT CURRY
Junglee pheasant kari

Pheasants seem to be in every field in Lincolnshire, so it's not surprising that some have made their way into our curries. Under all those feathers, pheasants are very lean birds, so it's best to cook them slowly on a gentle heat to keep the meat soft, and in a deep, rich sauce to complement their bold, gamey flavor. This dish is best served when it's cold outside and with something fresh or green, like a salad or some spinach.

SERVES 4 NORMAL OR 2 HEARTY EATERS

2 pheasants (around 3¼ pounds in total)

¼ cup unsalted butter

5 cloves

12 peppercorns

1 cinnamon stick

2 large onions, sliced

2-inch piece of ginger, peeled and grated

6 cloves of garlic, crushed

2 tablespoons ground coriander

2 teaspoons ground cumin

2 teaspoons ground cinnamon

2 teaspoons chili powder

1 teaspoon garam masala

4 ounces ground cashews (or ground almonds if these are easier to find)

1½ teaspoons salt

2 tablespoons tomato paste

½ cup whole-milk yogurt

2 14-ounce cans of plum tomatoes, crushed

a pinch of saffron

Pick over the pheasants to ensure they are free of shot and feathers, then rinse, pat dry, and set to one side. (This is not necessary if bought from a butcher.)

Put the butter into a casserole dish large enough to hold the pheasants, on a medium heat. When the butter starts to foam, add the cloves, peppercorns, and cinnamon stick. Stir-fry for 2 minutes, until you can smell them, then add the onions. Cook them for 10 to 12 minutes, until soft, golden, and starting to brown. Then add the ginger, garlic, coriander, cumin, ground cinnamon, chili powder, garam masala, cashews, and salt. Mix thoroughly.

Now add the tomato paste and the yogurt, followed by the canned tomatoes. Pour them out with one hand, crushing them with the other hand before they hit the pan. Fill up a tomato can with water and pour that into the casserole dish, too.

Lower in the pheasants, bring the mixture to a boil, then pop the lid on the casserole dish and turn the heat down to the lowest setting. Cook for around 1 to 1½ hours, turning the birds every now and then to ensure they cook evenly. To check that they're cooked through, poke with a skewer and if the juices run clear, take them off the heat.

When the pheasants are cooked, stir in the saffron. Taste the sauce and adjust the chili and salt if need be. To serve, cut the pheasant into portions and serve alongside some rice, greens, or a big side salad.

SLOW-COOKED LAMB AND SPINACH CURRY
Gosht anna palak nu shaak

This is one of my favorite springtime dishes. The warming lamb curry and just-wilted spinach are perfect for when there's still a nip in the air but you're hankering after something fresh. Slow-cooking the lamb shoulder breaks down the fat, which makes the meat wonderfully soft and helps create a rich, silky sauce.

I often make the lamb curry a day before serving to allow the flavors to deepen, then throw in the spinach the next day, just before serving.

SERVES 4

3 tablespoons canola oil

2 large onions, sliced

1¾-inch piece of ginger, peeled and grated

6 cloves of garlic, crushed

¾ teaspoon chili powder

1 tablespoon ground cumin

1 tablespoon ground coriander

1¾ pounds lamb shoulder, chopped into 1¼-inch cubes

1 14-ounce can of good-quality plum tomatoes

1 tablespoon tomato paste

1½ teaspoons salt

1 pound fresh baby spinach

Put the oil in a heavy-bottomed, lidded casserole dish on a medium heat. When it's hot, add the onions and fry for 10 to 12 minutes, until soft, golden, and starting to brown. Add the ginger and the garlic and cook for another 4 to 5 minutes, stirring.

Add the chili, cumin, and coriander, and follow with the diced lamb. When the lamb pieces have browned all over, add the plum tomatoes, pouring them into the pan with one hand and breaking them up with the other, then the tomato paste, and the salt. Stir well. Fill the tomato can with half as much water (¾ cup) and add that to the dish. Give it a final stir and bring the mixture to a boil, then cover with the lid and turn the heat down low. Simmer for around 1¼ hours, or until the meat is soft and tender.

When you're happy with the tenderness of the meat, add the spinach to the pot in batches and cook until just wilted. Leave the lid off to reduce the sauce to your desired consistency, then take off the heat.

This is especially good with a steaming bowl of caramelized onions and jeera rice (see page 155).

HOWRAH EXPRESS CINNAMON LAMB CURRY

Taj anna loving wari gosht

Lamb and cinnamon have always been natural flirts. Throw tomatoes in and you've got an ingredient love triangle. The result, and you need to give it time, is a rich and earthy dish with that mellow sweetness that only cinnamon can give.

I first ate this on the 26-hour train journey on the Howrah Express from Kolkata to Jaipur, crossing through the desert, cities, and villages. Here's my recreation, the taste of which takes me straight back to the wonders of the Indian railways.

I've used neck fillet, not only because it's relatively cheap, but also because it comes into its own when cooked long and slow, falling apart in your mouth as you eat it.

SERVES 8

4 tablespoons canola oil
2 large onions, finely chopped
8 cloves of garlic, finely chopped
1 14-ounce can of plum tomatoes
1½ teaspoons garam masala
1¼ teaspoons chili powder

2 teaspoons ground cumin
1½ tablespoons ground cinnamon
1½ teaspoons salt
2¼ pounds lamb neck fillet, chopped into
  1¼ x ¾-inch pieces
⅔ cup whole-milk yogurt, whisked

Put the oil into a large, heavy-bottomed casserole dish on a medium heat. When it's nice and hot, add the onions. Fry the onions until golden, which will take 8 to 10 minutes, then add the garlic. Stir-fry for another couple of minutes.

Next add the plum tomatoes. I tend to pour the canned tomatoes out using one hand and crush them using the other before they hit the pan. Cook the tomatoes for around 6 minutes, or until they have thickened, with little juice running from them.

Add the garam masala, chili powder, cumin, cinnamon, and salt, and mix. Once mixed, add the lamb and cook until the meat has browned all over. Add the yogurt a spoonful at a time, stirring slowly (to stop it splitting), and then add ¾ cup of warm water – there should be enough to just cover the lamb.

Bring the mixture to a boil, then cover with the lid, turn the heat down to low, and simmer for 1½ hours, or until the lamb is falling apart. Remove the pan lid to reduce the sauce to your desired consistency, then take off the heat.

Check for seasoning and serve with some hot flaky paratha (see page 198) or naan (see page 199), which you can use to mop up the lovely sauce.

LAMB KEBABS WITH CUMIN AND CORIANDER
Boti kebab

The smell of meat on a grill marks the start of summertime, but the smell of a barbecued kebab marks the start of our family summer. These lamb kebabs are marinated in some bold flavors and then charred to give a lovely smokiness. If it's not grilling season, then don't worry: this dish also works really well using a griddle or frying pan. You will also need some bamboo or metal skewers to make the kebabs.

SERVES 4

1¼ pounds lamb shoulder

1½-inch piece of ginger, peeled and roughly chopped

3 cloves of garlic, roughly chopped

salt

3 tablespoons canola oil

1½ teaspoons ground cumin

1½ teaspoons ground coriander

½ teaspoon chili powder

1 teaspoon ground cinnamon

8 grinds of the pepper mill

grated zest of 1 lemon

1 tablespoon lemon juice

If you're using bamboo skewers, soak them in cold water first for 30 minutes so that they don't catch fire when you cook.

Pick over the lamb shoulder for fat and sinew, cut the lamb into bite-size pieces (around 1 x 1-inch) and set aside in a large bowl. Put the ginger and garlic into a mortar and pestle and bash with a pinch of salt to form a paste. Make the marinade in another bowl by mixing together the oil, the ginger and garlic paste, the spices, a teaspoon of salt, the lemon zest, and lemon juice. Pour the marinade over the lamb pieces and mix well, getting in there with your hands to ensure they all make friends.

If using bamboo skewers, take them out of the cold water. Thread the lamb pieces onto your skewers and grill the lamb over a moderate heat for around 10 to 12 minutes, turning the kebabs every so often so that they cook evenly. If you don't have a grill, use a griddle pan or a heavy-bottomed frying pan on a high heat with a very small amount of oil and cook the kebabs for 8 minutes, turning them frequently so as not to burn the lamb. Whichever method you use to cook the kebabs, make sure to let them rest for 3 to 4 minutes before tucking in.

Serve with my pomegranate and mint raita (see page 188), toasted naan (see page 199), and kachumbar (see page 185).

SPICY LAMB BURGERS

This was originally my recipe for Indian shami kebab, but over time it has transformed into a burger because sometimes there really is nothing more joyful than wrapping both hands around a meat-filled sandwich and tackling it cobra-style. There's a real simple pleasure in making your own burgers too: just chop, mix, then fry.

This recipe uses chickpea flour (besan), which is readily available in most big supermarkets, but if you can't get hold of it then you can use all-purpose flour to bind your mixture instead. This burger goes particularly well with tomato chutney (see page 218) and baked masala fries (see page 176), both of which are quick to make.

SERVES 4

1 onion, very finely chopped

1 fresh green chili, finely chopped

3 tablespoons finely chopped cilantro

1¾-inch piece of ginger, peeled

2 cloves of garlic

¾ teaspoon salt

2 teaspoons garam masala

a few grinds of the pepper mill

1½ tablespoons chickpea flour (besan)

14 ounces ground lamb

1 tablespoon canola oil

To serve

4 white bread buns

7 ounces spinach leaves

1 large red onion, sliced into thin rings

2 large tomatoes, sliced into thin rings

Put the onion, green chili, and cilantro into a bowl. Grate the ginger and crush the garlic and add them, too. Then add the salt, garam masala, black pepper, chickpea flour, and ground lamb and use your hands to mix everything together.

Divide the mixture into four balls and flatten them into round patties with your hands. Put the oil into a non-stick pan on a medium to high heat and, when it's hot, add the patties. Cook for 5 to 6 minutes on each side.

To serve, split the buns and toast them in a toaster, or in a hot pan after brushing them lightly with oil. Place some spinach, onion, and tomato rings on one half of the buns, top with the burgers, and slather with tomato chutney. Cold beer optional.

MAHARANI'S FAVORITE
Slow-roasted lamb shoulder

This is an ode to my grandfather, a man who slow-cooked in his own way back in 1940s Uganda. He'd go hunting and return with an antelope, dig a hole to make an oven, wrap it in banana leaves, and cook it overnight until the meat fell apart.

It's hard to find antelope and I don't have a spade, so here is a dish that takes the spirit of what my grandfather created and brings it into the present. The name of this recipe comes from the way my grandfather used to treat my mum like a princess, a maharani, bringing her back many treasures from his travels, including his latest kill. This dish needs time, at least 4 hours of cooking, but the reward is pure pleasure.

SERVES 4 TO 6

1 tablespoon cumin seeds

1 teaspoon fennel seeds

1 teaspoon peppercorns

½ teaspoon ground cardamom (or finely ground seeds from 6 pods)

1 star anise

6 cloves

4 cloves of garlic, roughly chopped

2-inch piece of ginger, peeled and roughly chopped

1 level tablespoon salt

1 tablespoon ground cinnamon

½ teaspoon chili powder

juice of 1 lemon

3 tablespoons canola oil

1 large lamb shoulder (around 3½ pounds)

Preheat the oven to 275°F.

Put a large frying pan over a medium heat and dry-roast the cumin, fennel, peppercorns, cardamom, star anise, and cloves for 1 to 2 minutes, then grind together in a clean spice grinder or a mortar and pestle. Remove the spices and set to one side, then grind the garlic, ginger, and salt to a paste. Add to the spices, along with the cinnamon, chili powder, lemon juice, and oil.

With a sharp knife, make small cuts all over the lamb and rub in the spice paste. Marinate in the fridge for at least an hour and up to 8 hours. The longer, the better.

Put a large, heavy-bottomed, lidded casserole dish on a medium heat. When hot, place the lamb in it, fatty side up, pour in around ½ cup of warm water and pop the lid on. Put it in the oven to cook, basting it every hour for 4 hours and turning it over after 2 hours. After 4 hours the lamb should be falling apart nicely. If not, keep cooking it, checking it every 20 minutes or so until done, then take the casserole dish out of the oven.

Pour all of the juices into a pitcher. Turn up the oven to 400°F and pull the lamb off the bone, using a fork, and spread it out on the bottom of the casserole dish. When the oven is hot, put the lamb back in the oven for 20 minutes or until crisp.

Serve the lamb with its juices on the side along with hot buttered naan (see page 199), kachumbar (see page 185), and roasted cauliflower with cumin, turmeric, and lemon (see page 191).

LAMB RAAN

Alexander the Great was quite a man: educated by Aristotle; commander of the biggest empire in the world by the age of 30; and an able hand in the kitchen. Legend has it that on conquering India and dethroning King Paurava, Alexander became great friends with the ex-king. To recognize their new friendship, Paurava held the banquet to end all banquets, the centerpiece of which was a grilled and spiced leg of lamb: lamb raan.

This is a great dish befitting great guests; just be sure to start it the day before they arrive.

SERVES 6 TO 8 (A SMALL ARMY)

a large leg of lamb, around 5½ pounds
1½ teaspoons cumin seeds
1 tablespoon coriander seeds
1 teaspoon black peppercorns
seeds from 6 cardamom pods
1 cup whole-milk yogurt
6 cloves of garlic, crushed
3-inch piece of ginger, peeled and finely grated

1 cup ground almonds
juice of ½ lemon
1½ teaspoons chili powder
2 tablespoons ground cinnamon
2 teaspoons salt
14 ounces shallots
canola oil

The day before you want to serve the dish, score the leg of lamb with a sharp knife, making deep cuts in crosses on both sides, and set aside.

In a spice grinder, or mortar and pestle, grind the cumin, coriander seeds, black peppercorns, and cardamom together. Put the spices into a large bowl, and add the yogurt, garlic, ginger, almonds, lemon juice, chili powder, ground cinnamon, and salt.

Rub the marinade onto the lamb and into the grooves, then transfer to a large plastic food bag or a casserole dish and cover. Leave in the fridge overnight.

The next day, around 3 hours before you want to serve the lamb, preheat the oven to 350°F.

Transfer the lamb to a deep roasting tray, pour ½ cup of water into the tray, and loosely cover with foil. Cook for 2¼ hours for lamb that is pink in the middle, and 2½ hours if you like it more well done.

Forty-five minutes before the finished cooking time, add the unpeeled shallots to the pan and lightly drizzle with oil. With 20 minutes to go, remove the foil so that the lamb browns nicely. Take the meat out of the oven, cover with foil, and rest it for 15 to 20 minutes before carving.

Some great accompaniments to this are my spinach with black pepper, garlic, and lemon (see page 179), roasted cauliflower with cumin, turmeric, and lemon (see page 191), mint and yogurt chutney (see page 219), and naan (see page 199).

THE PERFECT LAMB BIRYANI
Badshah biryani

Biryani is the maharajah (king) of dishes and is believed to have been invented in the kitchens of the Mughal emperors. It's a layered dish combining a rich and tender clove and cinnamon lamb curry, sweet caramelized onions, and saffron-scented rice. Traditionally the biryani pot is covered with a bit of dough and baked in the oven until cooked. Few experiences match the joy of cracking through the top of a freshly cooked biryani at the table and inhaling the beautiful steam which billows out. That said, you could easily use a good oven pot with a tight-fitting lid instead.

This dish is very much suited to sharing at home with family and friends, and although there may seem a lot to do, it's really no more complicated than making a lasagna.

SERVES 8 TO 10

For the lamb curry

2 star anise

2 tablespoons coriander seeds

10 cloves, or ½ teaspoon ground cloves

50 black peppercorns

1 tablespoon cumin seeds

½ teaspoon cardamom seeds

1 teaspoon fennel seeds

1¾-inch cinnamon stick

4 large onions

2-inch piece of ginger, peeled

8 cloves of garlic

canola oil

2¼ pounds lamb shoulder, chopped into 1¼-inch cubes

½ teaspoon ground turmeric

½ teaspoon chili powder

3 tablespoons whole-milk yogurt

3 tablespoons tomato paste

salt

For the rice

2¾ cups basmati rice

1 teaspoon rose water

a large pinch of saffron, soaked in 2 tablespoons hot water

For the dough

¾ cup chapati flour

¼ cup hot water

1 teaspoon canola oil

There's a fair bit of preparation involved in this dish, but if you tackle it up front, you will have few complaints later. First prepare all your spices. Put the star anise, coriander, cloves, peppercorns, cumin, cardamom, fennel, and cinnamon stick into a spice grinder, food processor, or mortar and pestle to grind them, and then set the spice mix to one side.

Rinse your basmati rice in at least three changes of water to wash out the starch and let it soak in a bowl of cold water until later. Next, chop your onions in half, peel them, and then slice into fine rings. Pop the ginger and garlic into a food processor, or finely grate the ginger and crush the garlic.

Put a tablespoon of oil into a large, heavy-bottomed, lidded frying pan on a high heat. When you are sure that the pan is very hot, sear the lamb in batches (so that you don't crowd the pan), turning it until it is golden brown. Take the meat out with a slotted spoon and set aside.

Add another 2 tablespoons of oil to the same pan and fry the onions for 8 to 10 minutes, until they are soft and golden. Take out half of the onions, transfer them to a bowl and set to one side. Then put the garlic and ginger into the pan. Stir-fry for a couple of minutes and add the spices that you have ground, together with the turmeric and chili powder. Keep stirring to ensure these don't burn on the bottom of the pan.

After a minute or so, add the lamb, yogurt, and tomato paste, stir well to ensure it is all mixed together, and add 1½ cups of warm water. Bring to a boil, then turn the heat down to low, pop the lid on, and leave to simmer for around 1½ hours, or until done.

Meanwhile, you'll need to cook the rice and prepare the fried onions for layering. Drain the rice and transfer to a saucepan. Pour enough cold water over the rice so that it is covered by 1–2 inches, and bring to a boil. Boil for 8 to 10 minutes, until it's just tender. Drain and set aside.

Transfer the onions from the bowl to a small frying pan and continue to fry for another 10 minutes, or until the onions are caramelized, then take off the heat. Check on the lamb: as soon as it is falling apart, season with salt to taste and take off the heat. If you'd like to seal your biryani lid with dough, knead together the flour, hot water, and oil to make a nice soft dough. Alternatively you could seal the pot with a tight lid or foil.

Preheat the oven to 350°F.

Take an ovenproof pot which will snugly accommodate the rice and lamb, such as a casserole dish. Remove half of the meat from the lamb curry using a slotted spoon (to leave the sauce behind) and place it at the bottom of the pot. Top the meat with half of the rice and half of the onions and repeat with the rest of the meat, rice, and onions. Keep the sauce from the curry aside to serve with the biryani.

Sprinkle the rice with the rose water and the saffron. Roll out the dough so that it is big enough to cover the pot, then place it on the pot and seal by pressing down on the rim all the way around (or put the lid on). Put the pot in the oven for 20 minutes.

Crack open the biryani at the table and serve with the lamb curry sauce on the side, along with some golden garlic raita (see page 178) and, if you like, some pomegranate seeds and cilantro leaves.

FISH

04

FISH

Fish and seafood feature on most Indian restaurant menus, but their offerings tend to be fairly limited to the same old tandoori fish or jumbo shrimp dishes. Yet with so much coastline backing on to the deep blue Arabian Sea and the Indian Ocean, there are loads of delicious sea creatures and undiscovered fishy dishes on India's menu.

Mumbai, the city of Indian dreams, was founded by the Koli fisherfolk who first inhabited the islands to make the most of the coastal fish supplies. Even the city's rename from Bombay to Mumbai pays homage to the Hindu goddess Mumbadevi, who is said to watch over the fishing communities. To this day, as the horizon fills with skyscrapers and the population races past 17 million, the fisherfolk and noisy Crawford fish market are still central to the city. The most popular fish in the market is Bombay duck, or bombil, an ugly, wide-mouthed fish popularly fried but now endangered through indiscriminate fishing.

Travel south down the Konkan coast and you'll find gigantic crabs, buttered and peppered, then ray, shark, jumbo shrimp, oysters, and mussels, as well as tuna and red snapper. Often the seafood down the coast is cooked very simply: rubbed with ginger, garlic, chili, and butter, and grilled to perfection. Or doused in spices thick enough to form a fire-bellied sauce, like the famous Goan Xacuti curry.

Further south still, in Kerala, you can stop by a seaside café and choose your cut from a gargantuan, spear-nosed, shimmering blue marlin or a banana-leaf-wrapped kingfish and eat the famous coconut fish curry.

In the east, where Bengal is riddled with waterways, the passion for fish continues. A salmon-like fish, hilsa, and shrimp of a size I've never before seen reign supreme there. Bengalis steam their fish in mustard paste and cook them in a forest-green cilantro sauce or a rich, creamy tomato sauce.

In Uganda, Mum was raised in a village on the Nile. She's told me of a fish there called "gagae," which was cooked over an open fire with black pepper, chili, and salt. The Nile, she says, was much like the River Humber, which we grew up next to – but full of crocodiles and hippos with the odd giraffe, elephant, or zebra wandering by.

Gujaratis are traditionally vegetarian, but because I was brought up in an untraditional Gujarati family of adventurous fish-eaters we often wrestled with lobsters, declawed crabs, pulled the heads off shrimp, and committed many other sea-creature atrocities. As a consequence, many of our family recipes are either inspired mouthfuls that come from dishes all over India or are created from traditional Gujarati techniques that have been reapplied to fish.

I am lucky enough to have grown up near to one of the largest fishing docks in the country, Grimsby, and now live in London near a wonderful fishmonger's (Steve Hatt); when I am organized, I love stocking up on a dawn trip to Billingsgate fish market, too.

But one thing is certain: we can't consume fish carelessly these days without risking the future of fish we love. Whenever possible, always buy from sustainable sources and stocks.

CHILI-FRIED SQUID WITH SPINACH, TOMATO, AND CILANTRO SALAD

This squid dish is by far one of the simplest and most delicious in our fishy family repertoire. The key to this is to marinate the squid for as long as possible before quickly sautéing it.

SERVES 4

For the squid

canola oil

3 to 4 fat cloves of garlic, finely sliced

2 fresh red chilis, very finely chopped

1½ pounds prepared squid (about 4 medium squid)

salt, preferably sea salt

1 lime, quartered

For the salad

7 ounces cherry tomatoes, halved

5 ounces radishes, very finely sliced

½ red onion, very finely sliced

a big bunch of cilantro (1½ ounces), leaves chopped

14 ounces baby spinach, washed

2 tablespoons lime juice

3½ tablespoons canola oil

1¼ teaspoons sugar

¾ teaspoon salt

Prepare a dish for the squid to marinate in; a small flat dish with a rim would be perfect. Put 3 tablespoons of oil, the garlic, and the red chilis into it, and mix together.

Give each squid a good rinse under the cold tap and pat dry with paper towels. Pull the wings off the body of the squid and keep to one side, then take a sharp knife and cut down the "seam" of the body to open it out. Cut the body in half and lightly score a cross-hatch pattern on each side. Throw it into the marinade dish, along with the tentacles and wings, then prepare the other squid in the same way. Place the marinating squid in the fridge for 30 minutes to allow the flavors to mingle.

Meanwhile, prepare the salad by putting the tomatoes, radishes, onion, cilantro, and spinach in a bowl and mixing thoroughly. To make up the dressing, whisk the lime juice, oil, sugar, and salt together. Taste and adjust the seasoning if need be and set to one side.

Have a pair of tongs on hand and a plate on which to park the fried squid. Put a tablespoon of oil into a frying pan and, when the pan is really hot, add just enough squid so as to give each piece room. Season each piece with some sea salt and fry for a minute on each side. The squid will firm up, turn white, and curl up when cooked. Don't be tempted to take the squid off any sooner, and don't overcook it, as it will turn rubbery.

Generously squeeze over some lime, then add the squid to the salad, and drizzle over with the dressing. Serve with some garlic naan and a few beers.

COCONUT FISH CURRY
Fish moilee

Coconuts run amok in Kerala and there are plenty of fish in the sea. Bring them together and you have Kerala on a plate.

My favorite fish to use in this curry is hake because its strong, sweet flavor complements the delicate but luxurious coconut curry, but you could easily use any other firm white fish.

SERVES 4

2-inch piece of ginger, peeled and roughly chopped

4 cloves of garlic, roughly chopped

1 fresh green chili, roughly chopped
  (seeded if you prefer less heat)

salt

3 tablespoons coconut or canola oil

optional: 20 fresh curry leaves

2 medium onions, thinly sliced

2 big ripe tomatoes, quartered

¾ teaspoon ground turmeric

½ teaspoon chili powder

1 cup plus 2 tablespoons coconut milk

4 fillets (5–6½ ounces each) of MSC-
  certified firm white fish such as hake,
  pollack, haddock, or cod, skinned

1 lime, quartered

Put the ginger, garlic, and green chili in a mortar and pestle, along with a pinch of salt, and bash to a paste.

Put the oil into a wide-bottomed, lidded frying pan on a medium heat. When it's hot, add the curry leaves if you are using them, followed by the onions, and stir every now and then for 8 to 10 minutes, until the onions are pale gold. Add the ginger, garlic, and chili paste and cook for another 2 to 3 minutes. Then add the tomatoes, 1½ teaspoons of salt, the turmeric, and the chili powder. Put the lid on the pan and cook for a couple of minutes.

Meanwhile, dilute the coconut milk with ½ cup of water and add to the pan. When the milk starts to bubble, add the fish fillets, turn the heat down a little, cover with the lid, and cook for approximately 5 to 7 minutes, or until the fish is cooked through.

Serve with a big squeeze of lime and some rice.

CILANTRO AND CUMIN STUFFED SARDINES
Dhana jiru bhareli maachi

The joy of sardines is that you don't need to fiddle with them very much to make a lip-smacking supper. As good as they are on their own, they get even better with a very simple stuffing made from cilantro, garlic, and a little cumin.

Stuffing fish with this kind of lilli chatni, or fresh green chutney, is commonplace in India, but the fish there are more often grilled or pan-fried. I prefer to bake mine, because it's an easy and quick way to prepare a lot of sardines, but if you want to grill your sardines, lightly oil them and cook them for around 3 to 4 minutes on each side.

SERVES 4, ALONGSIDE SOME BREAD, CHUTNEY, AND SALAD

canola oil

12 large sardines

salt (preferably sea salt)

½ teaspoon ground turmeric

2 teaspoons cumin seeds

6 cloves of garlic, finely sliced

3 fresh green chilis, very finely sliced

juice of 1 lemon

½ teaspoon sugar

a really big bunch of cilantro (3½ ounces), leaves chopped

Preheat the oven to 400°F. Line and lightly oil a large oven tray or two for the fish.

Rinse the sardines under the cold tap, rubbing the bodies with your thumbs to remove the scales, or shuffle them off using the back of a knife. To gut the sardines, cut all the way along the belly, and scrape out the bits inside using your knife. Rinse the fish again under a tap. Sprinkle with salt and turmeric and rub both inside the body and out, then put in the fridge while you make the stuffing.

Bash up the cumin along with a pinch of salt in a mortar and pestle. Add the garlic and green chilis and roughly bash up. Drizzle in the lemon juice and 4 tablespoons of oil, add the sugar, mix together, and add the cilantro. Taste and adjust as you wish. You might want to add more heat, salt, or oil.

Rub the paste on the inside and outside of the fish. Line up the fish on your oven tray(s) and bake for 10 to 15 minutes until done.

Serve with fresh hot naan (see page 199), tomato chutney (see page 218), and chaat salad (see page 192).

20-MINUTE FISH CURRY
Pesi pesi maachi

Like most people, sometimes I need something really quick to make, without wasting time and without having to compromise on taste. This recipe is just that: a speedy fish curry with a depth of flavor that is surprising. Perfect to keep you company on a weekday night.

I use coley, a white fish which is less well known than its cousins haddock and cod, but just as versatile, and more sustainable and cheaper, too. Its sweet flavor and meaty texture go well with the cherry tomatoes in this curry. A quick tip: it's worth putting the rice on at the same time as you start cooking the curry.

SERVES 4

3 tablespoons canola oil

½ teaspoon mustard seeds

2 medium onions, finely sliced

4 cloves of garlic, crushed

14 ounces cherry tomatoes, halved

1 teaspoon chili powder

1 teaspoon ground coriander

1½ teapoons ground cumin

1 teaspoon salt

¾ cup hot water

1¼–1¾ pounds coley or cod (or any other firm white skinned, boned, and MSC-certified fish such as pollack), cut into 1¾-inch cubes

1 lemon, quartered

a small bunch of cilantro (1 ounce), finely chopped

Put the oil into a non-stick, lidded frying pan on a medium heat and, when it's hot, add the mustard seeds. Stir-fry for a couple of minutes, or until they pop, then add the onions and garlic. Cook for around 8 minutes, or until golden and soft, then add the cherry tomatoes.

Cover the pan with the lid and cook the tomatoes for around 4 to 5 minutes, until the mixture is looking paste-like. Now add the chili powder, the ground coriander, and cumin, the salt, and the hot water.

Wait for the liquid to start to bubble, then add the fish pieces. Stir gently into the sauce, cover with the lid, and cook for a further 3 to 4 minutes, or until cooked.

Serve with rice, a generous squeeze of lemon, and a scattering of cilantro.

GRIMSBY SMOKED HADDOCK KEDGEREE

This comforting dish, a version of kitchari (see page 159), dates back to when the British were in India and many dishes were adapted to suit more delicate palates, resulting in some fine culinary mishmashery. Unlike most kedgeree recipes, mine is not made with cream or milk. This recipe is for a light, flavor-packed kedgeree, using British smoked haddock and soft-boiled eggs on a bed of spiced lemony rice.

SERVES 4

2 cups basmati rice

2½ cups hot vegetable stock

1 pound skinless, undyed,
  MSC-certified smoked haddock fillets

3 tablespoons canola oil

2 medium red onions, finely sliced

4 cloves of garlic, very finely sliced

optional: ½ fresh green chili, very finely sliced

1¼ teaspoons garam masala

1½ teaspoons ground cumin

2 teaspoons ground coriander

1¼ teaspoons salt

¾ teaspoon ground black pepper

4 medium eggs at room temperature

½ cup peas (frozen or fresh)

1 tablespoon of ghee or butter

a big bunch of cilantro (1½ ounces)

lemon wedges, to serve

Note: If you don't fancy boiling the eggs midway, you can boil the eggs first, before you start cooking.

Rinse the rice a few times and let it soak in a bowl of cold water on one side. Pour the stock over the haddock in a shallow dish, cover tightly with plastic wrap, and leave to poach.

Put the oil into a large, lidded frying pan on a medium heat and, when it's hot, cook the onions for 8 to 10 minutes, until soft and golden. Add the garlic and cook for a couple more minutes, then add the green chili, if using, the garam masala, ground cumin, ground coriander, salt, and black pepper. Stir everything together and cook for another 2 to 3 minutes. Drain the rice and add it to the pan, then stir gently so as not to break the rice.

Pour the stock from the poaching haddock into the pan and bring it to a boil, then turn the heat down low and cover the pan. Let it simmer gently for 15 minutes. Meanwhile, attend to the eggs. Put them into a small pan and cover with cold water. Bring the water to a boil, then turn the heat down low and simmer for exactly 6 minutes. Take the eggs out and plunge them into cold water before peeling.

Check the haddock for bones, then flake it into large pieces and put aside. When the rice has been simmering for 15 minutes, gently stir in the haddock and peas and put the lid back on. Leave it to cook for a further 5 minutes, or until the rice is cooked and all the stock absorbed. Remove from the heat and let it stand for 5 minutes, then dot with ghee or butter.

Finely chop the cilantro and sprinkle over the kedgeree, then halve the eggs and lay them on top. Serve with wedges of lemon to squeeze over.

MUSSELS IN A COCONUT AND GINGER SAUCE

Mussels were something we were first introduced to on holidays in France. They are the kind of ingredient that cooks' dreams are made of: cheap, readily available, and, after an initial scrub and polish, cooked in under 5 minutes. Add a few Indian flavors and you have an astonishing dish, perfect for dunking flaky paratha into.

SERVES 4 AS A LIGHT SUPPER

2 pounds 2 ounces mussels

3 tablespoons canola oil

optional: 10 fresh curry leaves

2 medium onions, finely chopped

1 fresh red chili, very finely chopped

1¾-inch piece of ginger, peeled, then grated or finely chopped

8 cloves of garlic, crushed

1½ tablespoons tomato paste

1 teaspoon sugar

½ teaspoon salt

¾ teaspoon chili powder

1½ cups coconut milk

1-inch piece of ginger, peeled, then sliced into fine matchsticks

3 tablespoons finely chopped cilantro

Sort through the mussels, tapping any that are open to see if they close. Throw away the ones that remain open or any that are damaged. Pull off any beards and scrape off any barnacles using the back of a knife, then rinse in a couple of changes of water and leave them to soak in a large bowl of cold water.

Put the oil into a non-stick, lidded frying pan that is large enough to accommodate all the mussels (or two smaller lidded pans), on a medium heat. When it's hot, add the curry leaves if you are using them, followed by the onions, and cook for 8 to 10 minutes, until the onions are golden but not brown.

Add the red chili, grated ginger, and garlic, and cook for a further minute before adding the tomato paste, sugar, salt, and chili powder. Stir to mix, then add the coconut milk.

When the milk starts to bubble, add the mussels without their water (if you grab a handful at a time and shake them, you will leave any grit behind in the soaking water).

Put the lid on the pan and cook for a couple of minutes until the mussels open, then turn the heat off. Stir slightly to mix the mussels with the sauce. If there are any mussels which have not opened at this point, discard them. Add the matchsticked ginger. Cover and steam for another 2 to 3 minutes, then scatter with the cilantro before serving.

Serve with hot flaky paratha (see page 198) or any other bread suitable for mopping up the delicious sauce.

FISH IN A CILANTRO, COCONUT, AND MINT PARCEL

Patra ni macchi

This is a Parsi recipe which both Mum and I have adopted into our kitchens with great fondness. These little "parcels" of fish coated in lashings of coconut, cilantro, mint, lemon, and garlic are steamed until they smell magnificent. Serving them is sort of like giving people presents at the dinner table. Traditionally the parcel is made of banana leaves, but they're hard to come by, even in London, so in their place I use the humbler and easier-to-find parchment paper and cooking twine.

SERVES 4

a really big bunch of cilantro (3 ounces)

1½ ounces fresh mint, leaves picked

3 ounces desiccated coconut

juice of 1 lemon

6 cloves of garlic

2 teaspoons sugar

1½ fresh green chilis (seeded if you prefer less heat)

1 teaspoon cumin seeds

1¼ teaspoons salt

3 tablespoons canola oil

4 fillets (5–6½ ounces each) of MSC-certified firm white fish such as hake, cod, or haddock, skinned and checked for bones

lemon wedges, to serve

Preheat the oven to 350°F.

Whizz up all of the ingredients except for the fish in a blender or food processor. Taste for seasoning; it should be hot, sweet, lemony, and herby, with no one flavor dominating any other.

Lay out a square of parchment paper that is big enough to wrap one fish fillet in. Place the fillet in the middle and spoon a quarter of the mixture on top of the fish. Wrap the fish up into a parcel and tie together with cooking twine or tuck the folds of the parcel under the fish so it won't open, then repeat with the other fillets.

Bake for around 15 minutes, or until the fish flakes easily. Serve with wedges of fresh lemon to squeeze over and some chaat salad (see page 192).

JUMBO SHRIMP WITH GARLIC AND MUSTARD SEEDS

Lasan anna rai wara chingri

Many conversations I have with my mother center around food these days. She takes great pleasure in reminding me that as a child I refused to eat anything but shrimp or Heinz tomato soup.

This is how she would cook the shrimp – with a bit of garlic and a few black mustard seeds, which are one of the most regularly used spices in Gujarati cooking. Throwing the seeds into hot oil right at the start of cooking causes them to pop, like popcorn, which releases their nutty, mustardy flavors and adds a lovely gentle heat.

SERVES 2 AS A MAIN DISH OR 4 AS A SIDE

2 teaspoons mustard seeds

2 tablespoons unsalted butter

optional: 6 fresh curry leaves

5 cloves of garlic, crushed

¼ teaspoon salt

½ teaspoon chili powder

½ fresh red chili, very finely chopped

¼ teaspoon ground turmeric

11 ounces jumbo shrimp, shelled

½ lemon

2 scallions, very finely sliced,
   to garnish

Crush a teaspoon of the mustard seeds in a mortar and pestle until the black skins split to reveal their yellow insides. Put a non-stick frying pan on a medium heat and, when it's nice and hot, add the butter. When the butter foams, add a teaspoon of the whole mustard seeds and wait for them to pop. This should happen after around 20 seconds in a hot pan; if not, move on, as you don't want them to burn and taste bitter.

Add the curry leaves if you are using them and the garlic and stir-fry for a couple of minutes. Now add the cracked mustard seeds, the salt, chili powder, red chili, and turmeric to the pan and stir-fry for a few seconds. Add the shrimp and stir. It should only take a minute or so for them to turn pink; as soon as they do, take them off the heat.

Squeeze the lemon over the shrimp and garnish with the scallions. Eat with rice or chapatis (see page 196) and a hearty salad.

SALMON AND SPINACH CURRY

My mum scratches her head. "I don't remember eating a lot of fish in Kampala, although we did live near the water. They certainly didn't have salmon, though." "So how did this dish come about?" I ask. "You loved salmon, and so did your sister, Sonal, so I created it especially for you."

Some dishes don't need explanations. This is one of my favorites, and I'm sure it'll become one of yours.

SERVES 4

2 tablespoons canola oil

1 cinnamon stick

6 whole peppercorns

2 cloves

1 large onion, chopped

½ teaspoon brown sugar

8–9 ounces ripe tomatoes, roughly chopped

1¾-inch piece of ginger, peeled and finely grated

4 cloves of garlic, crushed

optional: 1 fresh green chili, finely chopped

¼ teaspoon garam masala

1 teaspoon ground cumin

1½ teaspoons ground coriander

¼ teaspoon ground turmeric

½ teaspoon chili powder

1¼ teaspoons salt

1 pound spinach leaves

14 ounces skinless, MSC-certified salmon fillets

Put the oil into a large, lidded frying pan on a medium heat. When it's hot, add the cinnamon stick, peppercorns, and cloves, and cook for 1 to 2 minutes, until they start to release their aromas.

Add the onion and brown sugar and cook for 12 to 15 minutes, until golden and caramelized. Stir in the tomatoes, put the lid on the pan and cook for 5 minutes or so, until the tomatoes begin to soften.

Add the ginger and garlic (and green chili if you would like a little more heat), and stir in the garam masala, cumin, coriander, turmeric, chili powder, and salt. Keep stirring to ensure the spices don't catch on the bottom of the pan. After around 8 minutes the mixture should start to look quite paste-like. When it does, add the spinach, turn down the heat, and pop the lid back on and leave it to wilt.

Cut the salmon into big chunks, around 2 ½ x 2 ½ inches, and add to the pan. Coat the salmon in the tomato and spinach sauce, taking care not to break up the salmon pieces. Put the lid back on and leave for around 5 to 7 minutes, so that the fish cooks through.

Remove the cinnamon stick and check for seasoning. Serve with chapatis (see page 196) or my caramelized onions and jeera rice (see page 155).

EGGS

In the Western world, eggs are only really allowed out on their own at breakfast time. For the rest of the day they tend to be hidden away in cakes, soufflés, and pies. In India they're eaten throughout the day as a cheap, nutritious source of protein and a substitute for meat, or as a perfect snack (often boiled and sprinkled with black salt, dried mango powder, and pepper). Although there are not many recipes in this chapter, the few that are here are the select elite – my favorites.

For breakfast our dish of choice was always masala omelette (see page 148), usually eaten on a late Sunday morning along with buttered toast and ketchup and with some fresh chai (see page 260) to drink, decanted into a flowery china teapot. Even now, the smell of the omelette takes me back to my childhood in an instant.

Sometimes I will cheat on that memory, though, and eat Bombay eggs (see page 145) for brunch, a dish in which eggs are poached in tomatoes, crushed cumin, and cilantro. I adopted the recipe from Parsi friends in Mumbai who are known egg-o-philes and will take any opportunity to eat "kasa par ida" – "eggs on anything."

Eggs appeared as snacks in our family in the form of inda boflo (see page 147) – essentially a spiced eggy bread which was made for my mother and her brothers by my grandma, and also for me and my sister by my mum, when we were growing up in our little Lincolnshire village.

If it is dinner, it has to be a caramelized onion, coconut, and egg curry (see page 146). Sweet onions swaddle the eggs in a creamy but piquant cinnamon, coconut, and tamarind sauce. It is a dream of a meal, inspired by a dish I ate in Kerala and Sri Lanka and which I regularly recreate at home.

BOMBAY EGGS

This is an old Parsi recipe. If you know a Parsi, you're lucky, as they're a rare bunch these days. Persecuted in Iran in the tenth century for their religion, Zoroastrianism, they fled and landed in Gujarat, adopting the local language (our very own Gujarati) but keeping their own religion and their food traditions.

Parsis worship fire, believe in "good words, good thoughts, and good deeds" and are eaten by vultures after they die. They also happen to love eggs, and I love this dish as a delicious, one-pot breakfast, served with some yogurt and hunks of bread for mopping up the tomatoey juices.

SERVES 4

1 teaspoon cumin seeds

2 teaspoons coriander seeds

4 tablespoons canola oil

1½ large onions, finely sliced

4 cloves of garlic, crushed

1¼-inch piece of ginger, peeled, then finely chopped or grated

2 pounds 3 ounces juicy ripe tomatoes, chopped

1 tablespoon tomato paste

1 teaspoon salt (or to taste)

1 teaspoon sugar

½ teaspoon chili powder

¼ teaspoon ground turmeric

8–9 ounces fresh spinach

6 medium eggs at room temperature

ground black pepper

a small bunch of cilantro (1 ounce), leaves chopped

1 cup homemade or Greek yogurt

In a large, lidded saucepan, toast the cumin and coriander seeds over a medium to high heat, swirling the pan around until the spices are a pale golden brown. It should take 2 to 3 minutes. Then lightly grind them in a mortar and pestle.

Pour the oil into the pan on a medium heat and, when it's hot, put the spices back into the pan. Stir-fry for a minute, then add the onions. Cook for 6 to 8 minutes, until they're starting to turn golden, then add the garlic and ginger. Cook for another couple of minutes before adding the chopped tomatoes.

Let the tomatoes cook and reduce for around 15 minutes, stirring occasionally, until they have thickened into a rich, bright sauce. Then add the tomato paste, salt, sugar, chili powder, and turmeric, mix well, and leave for a minute. Add the spinach, handful by handful, mix again, and leave the spinach to wilt in the sauce.

To bake the eggs, have them all ready to crack and put into the pan in quick succession. Make your first egg-sized well in the tomato sauce using the back of a wooden spoon and crack an egg into it. Then repeat as quickly as you can for the other eggs and put the lid on the pan. Turn the heat down really low and cook for 10 minutes, or until the whites of the eggs are set but the yolks still creamy.

Serve immediately with a sprinkling of pepper, the cilantro, a dollop of yogurt, and some hunks of bread.

CARAMELIZED ONION, COCONUT, AND EGG CURRY

Inda nu shaak

In this dish, soft-boiled eggs snuggle up to sweet, caramelized onions and bed down in a tamarind-flavored coconut sauce. The recipe came to my kitchen by way of a Keralan cook called Kirti, who made it for me every day when I stayed in Kollam. Just as I was wolfing down my final one, I begged him to show me how to cook it so I could take the recipe home with me. Happily, he obliged, and I find myself craving this on a regular basis here in London, when nothing else will do.

SERVES 4

3 tablespoons canola oil

2 onions, finely sliced

8 medium eggs at room temperature

6 cloves of garlic, crushed

1 teaspoon tamarind paste

¾ teaspoon chili powder

¾ teaspoon sugar

1¼ teaspoons salt

½ teaspoon ground turmeric

1 cup plus 2 tablespoons coconut milk
  mixed with ½ cup water*

Note: If you don't fancy juggling the boiling of the eggs with making the sauce, you can either boil the eggs before or after making the sauce.

Put the oil into a large, deep-sided frying pan on a medium heat and, when it's hot, add the onions. Fry them for 15 to 20 minutes, until brown and caramelized.

While the onions are cooking through, put the eggs into a large saucepan, cover generously with water, and bring to a boil. When the water comes to a boil, turn the heat down to a simmer and set a timer for exactly 6 minutes for just-set hard-boiled eggs.

Add the garlic to the onions, stir well and cook for another 2 to 3 minutes. Add the tamarind paste, chili powder, sugar, salt, and turmeric, stir-fry for a minute, then pour in the diluted coconut milk. Bring the mixture to a boil and turn down to a simmer.

When the eggs have finished boiling, plunge them into cold water for a couple of minutes, then peel them. Rinse, halve them, and fold into the coconut sauce, then take the pan off the heat.

Serve on a bed of rice or with paratha (see page 198) or chapatis (see page 196).

* Use the leftover ½ cup of coconut milk in a standard can to make the 100 garlic-clove curry (see page 62), or mix it into dal (see page 166) to make it rich and creamy, or freeze it in a freezer bag until next time.

INDA BOFLO
Spiced Ugandan eggy bread

"Inda" means "eggs" in Gujarati, and "boflo" means "bread" in Swahili. This is essentially an Indian version of French toast, but it's not stolen from the French, nor from the 1980s. My grandma used to make this for my mum and her brothers in 1950s Uganda as an after-school snack. When I have children, as sure as eggs are eggs, I'm going to make them this snack too.

SERVES 4 HUNGRY CHILDREN (OR ADULTS)

4 eggs
5 tablespoons milk
a big pinch of salt
½ teaspoon chili powder

a small bunch of cilantro
 (1 ounce), finely chopped
4 teaspoons canola oil
4 slices of bread

Crack the eggs into a large bowl. Whisk well, then add the milk, salt, chili powder, and cilantro, and mix together.

Put a teaspoon of oil into a frying pan on a medium heat. When the pan is nice and hot, quickly dip a slice of bread into the egg mixture (making sure it's coated on both sides) and place in the pan. Cook for around a minute on each side, until firm and browning in spots. Repeat with the rest of the bread and egg mixture.

Serve with tomato chutney (see page 218) or tomato ketchup.

MASALA OMELETTE

Masala amlet

This is the smell of Sunday morning in our family home. I would follow my nose like a cartoon wolf, down the stairs and into the kitchen, where this tasty omelette would be waiting alongside a pile of hot buttered toast, a fresh pot of chai, and Lata Mangeshkar's timeless, syrupy voice on the stereo.

SERVES 4

8 eggs

3 scallions, finely chopped

1 fresh green chili, finely chopped
(seeded if you prefer less heat)

a small bunch of cilantro (1 ounce),
finely chopped

½ teaspoon ground turmeric

1 teaspoon chili powder

¼ teaspoon salt (or to taste)

4 teaspoons canola oil

Break the eggs into a large bowl and lightly whisk until the yolks and whites are mixed. Add the scallions, green chili, and cilantro, along with the turmeric, chili powder, and salt, and mix together.

Put a teaspoon of oil into a frying pan (a 7–8 inch-diameter pan is ideal) on a medium heat. When it's hot, pour in a quarter of the omelette mixture and swirl it around the pan so that the bottom is coated, then leave for a minute or so. The egg should be cooked through but a bit soft on top. Flip it over for 30 seconds or so, before shuffling it out onto a plate.

Serve by itself, or between 2 pieces of buttered toast, with some ketchup and a Bollywood soundtrack in the background.

LEGUMES

06

GRAINS

LEGUMES AND GRAINS

Ask any Indian what their favorite food is, and they will most likely tell you that it's their mother's dal-bhaat (dal and rice). It might sound humble, but in the hands of an Indian cook these simple ingredients are transformed into food for the soul.

By far the most popular dal, and perhaps the most commonly eaten meal in India, is made from the red lentil (masoor dal), which is used in my mother's daily dal (see page 166). It's a comfort blanket of a meal: gingery and warming, and something which I make all winter long. Happily, it is also very robust; you could endlessly throw spices and ingredients at it and never go wrong.

A lesser-known dal, but the best I've ever eaten, is the dal makhani (see page 167), which is made with black lentils (urad dal). It's one of the most luxurious dishes in this book; as black as night, it's creamy and smoky, with a complexity that belies its simple list of ingredients, and it casts a spell over anyone who eats it. It's made using one of my favorite cooking methods too, one in which you leave the pot on a low simmer on the stove for a couple of hours and stir when passing.

Although no two dals are the same (see my note on lentils on page 297), most dal recipes are very easy to prepare. They usually require the lentils to be boiled, much like pasta, and then either cooked with tomatoes, ginger, onions, and garlic (India's favorite ingredients) to create bold flavors, or seasoned with a tarka – a spice-infused hot oil – for a simpler meal.

My mother tells me that our family ate more legumes and beans in Uganda, as they grow feverishly there. My father's favorite dish, junjaro (see page 168), a silken, spiced stew made with fat, buttery kidney beans, comes from their days in Africa. He can eat two portions in the blink of an eye, and will spend the rest of dinner excitedly recounting stories of his youth, of playing barefoot cricket on the dusty Ugandan earth, and dreaming of my mother.

We tend to eat all these lentils and beans with rice, although that isn't rice's only role. Often, all that is needed to elevate it from a humble grain is a cinnamon stick, a few cloves, and some butter (see the pilau on page 156), or some choice ingredients like dill (see page 158) or wild mushrooms (see page 170).

While cooking rice strikes fear into many cooks, a few tips and tricks are all you need to make perfect fluffy rice every time (see page 152).

Whatever you do with legumes and grains, you can't really go wrong. They are some of the most nourishing things you can put into your body. Resilient and forgiving, they will take whatever flavor you throw at them and reward you handsomely in return. Before you know it, dal will soon be the dish you can't do without (even if your mother never cooked it for you).

Some grains of wisdom on cooking the perfect rice

Opening a pan of freshly cooked basmati rice and watching as the billowing fragrant steam clears to reveal fluffy, separated long grains standing at attention is a magnificent wonder. I sometimes eat it on its own, with just a bit of salt and butter, and doing so is very rewarding.

But the task of cooking perfect rice has many adept cooks clenching their buttocks in utter fear, which is curious seeing as it is the staple food for most of the planet. If this sounds like you, fret no more. Here are some rules which will help you to cook perfect rice.

1st rule: one handful is enough for one person

These days, in the home, most Indian women use one mug's worth of rice to feed four people (which is around four handfuls and roughly equivalent to an 8-ounce cup). These are useful points to remember if you're ever cooking without measuring cups on hand. They also add a couple of extra handfuls for unexpected guests. I do the same, and if no one turns up it means there is enough for lunch the next day.

2nd rule: every portion of rice needs one and a half times the volume of water to cook in

This means that one mug of rice (which will feed four people) will require one and a half mugs of water to cook in. Easy.

3rd rule: rinse, soak, then cook

Rinsing and soaking will remove all the starch that causes grains of rice to stick together, helping to make them fluffy, and will also reduce the cooking time. Soaking rice in cold water for 30 minutes is perfect, but if you don't have that long, you can soak it for 10 minutes in warm water. I start to soak my rice just before I begin to cook a main meal.

4th rule: don't throw away the flavor

While there are generally a couple of different ways to cook rice, I use the absorption method (i.e. just enough water to cook the rice), because it means you don't rob the rice of all its delicious flavor by draining it down the sink.

5th rule: keep the lid on

When cooking rice, never open the lid, as it lets the steam out and that is what the rice is cooking in. If this means using a glass-lidded pan, so that you can peep at it without lifting the lid, so be it.

6th rule: give it 10 minutes off the heat

Always leave your rice to stand after cooking for around 10 minutes with the lid on. For some inexplicable reason, this makes the grains separate and stand up straight. Fluff with a fork before serving, and chuck in a pat of butter for good measure.

Always follow these golden rules and you won't go far wrong.

The six rules of rice

1. One handful is enough for one person

2. Every portion of rice needs one and a half times the volume of water to cook in

3. Rinse, soak, then cook

4. Don't throw away the flavor

5. Keep the lid on

6. Give it 10 minutes off the heat

THE PERFECT BASMATI RICE

TO FEED 4 PEOPLE, ALONGSIDE A MAIN DISH

1 cup of basmati rice
1½ cups of just-boiled water
2 tablespoons canola oil
¾ teaspoon salt

Wash the rice in a few changes of cold water, until the water runs clear. Let it soak in a bowl of cold water for at least 20 minutes, then drain. Put the kettle on to boil.

Put the oil into a wide-bottomed, lidded frying pan on a medium heat. Add the drained rice and the salt, stirring a couple of times, so as to coat each grain in the oil.

Pour in the boiling water and bring the rice to a fierce boil, then pop the lid on and turn the heat down to a simmer. Leave to cook for 10 minutes without lifting the lid.

If you have a clear lid, you'll see craters start to form in the rice where the water is bubbling through. Over time the number of bubbles will reduce, which is a sign that the water is being absorbed. If you're worried about there not being enough water, you can tip the pan. If the rice slides, you will know there's still water left on the bottom.

When the 10 minutes is up, turn the heat off and let the rice rest for a further 10 minutes. Just before serving, dot the rice with a couple of teaspoons of butter if you like, and gently fluff it up with a fork.

THREE WAYS WITH RICE

Caramelized onions and jeera rice
Dungree anna jiru waro bhat

The fragrance of freshly cooked jeera rice fills the whole house when it's cooked. This simple rice dish is lovely enough to eat by itself, but it's also a particularly good accompaniment to fish or dal.

SERVES 4, AS A SIDE

1 cup of basmati rice
2 tablespoons canola oil
1 large onion, finely sliced

1 teaspoon cumin seeds
1 teaspoon salt
1½ cups of just-boiled water

Wash the rice in 3 to 5 changes of cold water, until it runs clear, then leave to soak in a bowl of cold water for 20 minutes (or at least 10 minutes in warm water if you're stuck for time).

Put the oil into a wide-bottomed, lidded frying pan on a medium heat. When it's hot, fry the onion for 12 to 15 minutes, until just turning a rich dark brown, then add the cumin seeds and salt.

Boil the kettle. Drain the rice, add it to the onions, and stir well, making sure that you coat the grains with oil.

Pour over the boiled water. Stir, put the lid on, and bring to a rolling boil. After 2 minutes, turn the heat down to a simmer and cook for 10 minutes without lifting the lid no matter how tempting it might be.

Take off the heat and let it rest for 10 minutes to allow the steam to carry on cooking the rice. Fluff up with a fork and add a pat of butter if you like.

Cinnamon and clove pilau with cashew nuts
Taj, loving anna kaju waru pilau

"Pilau" means that the rice is cooked in a lovely flavored stock. This dish is one of the simplest flavored rices you can make: just a stick of cinnamon and a few cloves infuse the rice to create a beautifully delicate flavor.

SERVES 4, AS A SIDE

1 cup of basmati rice

2 tablespoons unsalted butter

1 cinnamon stick, broken in two

4 cloves

2 cups hot vegetable stock

a small handful of cashews

Wash the rice in 3 to 5 changes of cold water, until it runs clear, then let it soak in a bowl of cold water for 20 minutes (or at least 10 minutes in warm water if you're stuck for time). Drain and set aside.

Put the butter into a wide-bottomed, lidded frying pan on a medium heat. When the butter has melted, add the cinnamon stick and the cloves. Stir for 2 minutes, until you can smell the spices, then add the rice to the pan. Stir well, making sure that you coat the grains with butter.

Pour over the hot stock, stir again, and bring to a rolling boil. After 2 minutes, turn the heat down to a simmer, put the lid on, and cook for 10 minutes, without lifting the lid. Take off the heat and let it rest for around 10 minutes to allow the steam to carry on cooking the rice.

Open the lid, add a little more butter if you wish, fluff up with a fork, and scatter with the cashew nuts. Don't forget to fish out the pieces of cinnamon stick.

Steamed buttery rice with dill
Sua wara bhat

Dill used to grow in my grandma's garden in Porbandar, Gujarat. Just a small amount gives rice a lovely fresh pine flavor that works really well with both chicken and fish dishes. It's a great way to add a lot of flavor without much effort.

SERVES 4, AS A SIDE

1 cup of basmati rice

2 tablespoons unsalted butter

½ teaspoon salt

1½ cups of just-boiled water

1 ounce fresh dill

½ lemon

Wash the rice in 3 to 5 changes of cold water, until it runs clear, then leave to soak in a bowl of cold water for 20 minutes (or at least 10 minutes in warm water if you're stuck for time). Drain and set aside.

Boil the kettle to ensure you have hot water on hand. Put the butter into a wide-bottomed, lidded frying pan on a medium heat. When the butter has melted, add the salt and the drained rice. Stir well, making sure that you coat the grains with the butter, then pour over the boiled water.

Stir again and bring to a rolling boil, then put the lid on the pan, turn the heat down to a simmer, and cook for 10 minutes, without lifting the lid. Take off the heat and let it rest for around 10 minutes to allow the steam to carry on cooking the rice.

Tear up the dill, gently stir it through, then squeeze some lemon juice over the top. You can add an extra pat of butter, too, if you like.

BADSHAH KITCHARI

Kitchari is an ancient dish that is said to have inspired the British Indian kedgeree, together with the Egyptian kushari – now an incredibly popular street food in Egypt.

Traditional kitchari is a simple meal made of rice and lentils and eaten for dinner after a heavy lunch. But my mum makes a gorgeous, flavorful version of it, studded with good stuff like nuts, onions, garlic, and whole spices – hence the name "badshah kitchari," which means "the kitchari of kings."

SERVES 4

1¼ cups basmati rice

3 ounces split mung beans (moong dal) (or yellow split peas or red lentils if these are easier to find)

3 tablespoons ghee or unsalted butter

2-inch cinnamon stick

4 cloves

1 teaspoon cumin seeds

2 onions, thinly sliced

1 fresh green chili, finely chopped

4 cloves of garlic, crushed

1 teaspoon salt

½ teaspoon ground turmeric

3 cups hot vegetable stock

Combine the rice and mung beans or lentils and wash in a few changes of cold water, until it runs clear. Let them soak in a bowl of cold water for at least 30 minutes and up to 1 hour.

Put the ghee into a wide-bottomed, lidded, non-stick frying pan on a medium heat. When the ghee starts to foam, add the cinnamon stick, cloves, and cumin. Stir them around for 2 minutes, or until their smell fills the kitchen. Then add the onions and cook for 8 to 10 minutes, until soft and golden.

Add the green chili and garlic and cook for a further 2 minutes, then add the salt and turmeric. Drain the rice and lentils and add these to the pan, too. Pour in the hot stock and bring to a boil, then put the lid on the pan and turn the heat down to a simmer.

Cook until the water is absorbed, which should be around 25 minutes. Leave it to rest for at least 5 minutes with the lid on, then fluff up the rice with a fork.

Serve in individual bowls with a scattering of chopped cashews and almonds, some garlic pickle (see page 217), and a dollop of yogurt.

POMEGRANATE AND FENNEL SEED POHA

Daram anna valiary pawa

Poha is a cook's secret weapon. It's rice, but it cooks in just 5 minutes: as it's flattened and beaten, you only need to dunk it in some cold water before throwing it into your dish. You can buy it in Indian markets or order it online.

I first ate this poha for breakfast on a rooftop in Udaipur in Rajasthan when I was weary after an overnight train ride from Jaipur, across the desert. The next morning I asked Chef Suresh to teach me to make it and was really surprised to see just how easy it was.

This dish would make an excellent lunch or brunch. You might be able to find poha under its pseudonyms "flattened rice" or "beaten rice" in the supermarket or in an Indian grocer's shop.

SERVES 4

2 tablespoons canola oil
½ tablespoon fennel seeds
1 teaspoon mustard seeds
1 large red onion, finely sliced
7 ounces thick poha
1 teaspoon ground turmeric

1 teaspoon salt (or to taste)
a handful of garden peas (frozen are fine)
juice of 1 lemon
seeds of ½ pomegranate
⅓ cup sev (see page 308) or Bombay mix
a big bunch of cilantro (1 ounce), chopped

Put the oil into a wide-bottomed, lidded frying pan on a medium heat and, when it's hot, add the fennel and mustard seeds. When the mustard seeds start to pop, add the onion and fry for around 12 minutes, until lightly caramelized.

Meanwhile, put the poha into a sieve and gently rinse under cold water for a few minutes, until the water runs clear, then drain and set aside.

Once the onion is caramelized, add the turmeric, salt, and peas. Stir well and cook for 2 minutes, then add the drained poha and cover with the lid. Cook for a further 5 minutes. Check the poha is cooked through and not raw (it should be soft but with some bite, like cooked pasta), then take it off the heat.

To finish, squeeze the lemon juice over the poha and check the salt. Pop on to a plate and garnish with the pomegranate seeds, sev, and chopped cilantro.

CHANA DAL WITH GOLDEN GARLIC TARKA

Lasan anna chana dal

Chana dal, otherwise known as chickpea lentils, come from splitting and skinning black chickpeas (the most popular variety in India). Because they belong to the chickpea family, they're naturally very delicious and need little teasing before they turn into a gorgeous-tasting dal.

A tarka is a hot oil that is flavored with spices, garlic, and/or chili; it is added right at the end of a dish to enrich it. I've used golden garlic in this recipe, made by browning sliced garlic cloves to release their sweetness and depth.

SERVES 4

14 ounces chana dal (or yellow split peas if these are easier to find)

4 tablespoons canola oil

1 tablespoon cumin seeds

1 large onion, thinly sliced

6 cloves of garlic, thinly sliced

1 teaspoon garam masala

½ teaspoon chili powder

1 teaspoon salt (or to taste)

½ teaspoon mustard seeds

2 fresh red chilis, pricked with a knife in several places

Rinse the dal in a couple of changes of cold water, until the water runs clear, and then put in a saucepan. Pour in 5¼ cups of cold water, bring to a boil, and simmer for around 40 minutes, or until cooked. You'll know it's cooked because the lentils will become soft, with no bite or chalky texture. Scum will appear while you're boiling, which is completely normal; just remove it using a spoon and top up the water if necessary.

Put 2 tablespoons of oil into a frying pan on a medium heat and, when it's hot, add the cumin seeds, followed by the onion. Cook for around 15 minutes, until the onion has caramelized, then add half of the garlic and fry for a couple of minutes.

Add this mixture to the dal, along with the garam masala, chili powder, and salt. Taste and adjust any seasoning as you see fit. Add water to adjust the consistency to your liking, then transfer the dal to whatever you're serving it in.

For the final flourish, make the garlic tarka. Carefully wipe the frying pan clean with some paper towels and put it on a medium heat. Add the remaining 2 tablespoons of oil, followed by the mustard seeds. When they pop, add the rest of the garlic and the red chilis. Watch you don't cook the garlic for too long, as it will taste bitter. The very moment the edges of the garlic start to turn golden, take it off the heat and drizzle the tarka over the dal, placing the chilis on top as a garnish.

Stir through at the table and serve alongside rice, chapatis (see page 196), and some pickles.

DAILY DAL
Masoor dal

My mum and dad got married in 1975. At the wedding, Dad wore flares, platforms, and sideburns, and Mum wore a red sari. They moved to a bedsit in west London with a shared kitchen and a single cupboard. Mum would cook this dal then, and she still cooks it now.

This is one of my most treasured recipes: I crave it frequently and never tire of it. It's a foolproof dish, robust and endlessly adaptable, and it yields a result far greater than the effort required to make it (see photo on preceding page).

SERVES 4

8 ounces red lentils
2 tablespoons canola oil
optional: 12 peppercorns
optional: 4 cloves
1 onion, thinly sliced
4 cloves of garlic, crushed

2½-inch piece of ginger, peeled and finely grated
½ teaspoon chili powder
½ teaspoon ground coriander
½ teaspoon ground turmeric
1 teaspoon salt
11 ounces canned plum tomatoes

In a sieve, rinse the lentils until the water runs clear, then drain and put into a deep, lidded saucepan. Add 2½ cups of cold water, bring to a boil over a medium to high heat, then cover with the lid and simmer gently for 10 to 15 minutes without stirring, until thoroughly cooked. Like pasta, lentils will be tender when cooked.

Meanwhile, put the oil into another deep, lidded saucepan on a medium heat. When it's hot, add the peppercorns and cloves if you're using them. Stir-fry for around a minute, or until you can smell them, then add the onion. Cook for 8 to 10 minutes, until golden.

Add the garlic and ginger and stir-fry for a further 4 minutes before adding the chili powder, coriander, turmeric, and salt. Stir well, then add the canned tomatoes. If they're whole, pour them out with one hand and crush them with your other hand to break them up before they hit the pan. Cover, turn the heat down, and simmer for around 8 minutes.

The tomatoes should be looking darker and more paste-like now, with little tomato juice running from them. Add the lentils using a straining spoon, then pour in any remaining water they were boiling in, a little at a time, until you get a good consistency. For me, this is a fairly thick dal, thick enough to be eaten from a plate with bread, but you may prefer yours to be more soupy.

Finally, cover the pan with the lid again and cook on a low heat for a further 10 minutes.

Taste and adjust the salt, chili, or consistency as you see fit, and serve with chapatis (see page 196), homemade yogurt, and some garlic pickle (see page 217), or fire-bellied garlic and chili chutney (see page 220). Remember to watch out for the cloves and peppercorns.

DAL MAKHANI
Black dal

This is a recipe for one of the world's finest dishes. It takes exactly 142 minutes and 47 stirs to make, and it is worth every single one. Give it time and it will reward you handsomely with the most captivating, indulgent dal you've ever eaten, full of earthy, smoky flavors, rich deep tomato and warm buttery notes.

You'll need to soak the dal the night or morning before you want to eat it (6 hours is fine), and put it on the stove on a low heat a couple of hours before eating. Ask anyone passing by to give it a stir. This dal can also be made a day in advance.

SERVES 8

14 ounces urad dal (black lentils)

4 tablespoons unsalted butter, plus 2 tablespoons to finish

2 large onions, finely sliced

1¾-inch piece of ginger, peeled and finely chopped

10 cloves of garlic, crushed

6 tablespoons tomato paste

1¾ teaspoons salt

¾ teaspoon chili powder (or to taste)

1½ cups whole milk

In a sieve, rinse the urad dal in a couple of changes of cold water, until the water runs clear, then drain and put into a deep pan – they will double in volume while soaking. Cover with a generous amount of just-boiled water and let them soak for at least 6 and up to 24 hours.

Once they've finished soaking, rinse them, drain, and put back into the pan. Cover them with cold water and bring to a boil, then continue boiling for 45 minutes. Scrape off any scum that forms on the top and discard.

Meanwhile, put 4 tablespoons butter into a frying pan on a medium heat. When it starts to foam, add the onions and cook for 15 minutes, then add the ginger and garlic. Fry for another 5 minutes. It's not worth skimping on the time here: the longer you cook these (without burning), the more flavorful your dal will be. Add the tomato paste, salt, and chili powder, stir well, then take off the heat and set aside.

Once boiled, the dal should be soft enough to crush against the side of the pan. When it is done, keep enough water in the pan to just cover them and drain the rest off. Add the onion and tomato mixture and the milk, bring to a boil, then turn the heat down to a simmer.

Stir every now and then for around 1½ hours. If the sauce starts to run low, over time, top it up with an equal mixture of whole milk and water. The sauce will start to turn darker, richer, and creamier. If the dal is not rich and dark after 1½ hours, give it some more time – you can't do this dish any harm by cooking it for a little longer.

Taste, adjust the salt and chili, if necessary, add the remaining 2 tablespoons butter just before serving, and stir. Serve alongside rice or hot fluffy naan (see page 199).

JUNJARO
Kidney bean curry

There are only two occasions when my parents speak Swahili at home. The first is when they don't want me and my sister to know what's going on. The second is in the kitchen. After much confusion, I realized this was due to the brilliant cook that my mother's family in Uganda had, which meant that any conversations about that day's shopping list or dinner had to happen in Swahili. To this day, most conversations about food bounce between Gujarati, Swahili, and English.

One of my favorite Swahili words is "junjaro," which is the name of my dad's favorite kidney bean stew. It's a lovely blend of creamy smooth kidney beans, gently seasoned with ginger, garlic, tomatoes, and cumin.

Soak the kidney beans the night or morning before you want to eat them. You can use 14 ounces of canned kidney beans instead, which will make for a much quicker (30-minute) meal, but the dried kidney beans when cooked are bigger, softer, and tastier.

SERVES 4

7 ounces dried kidney beans (soaked overnight) or 2 14-ounce cans of kidney beans

2 tablespoons canola oil

1 cinnamon stick

½ teaspoon cumin seeds

1 large onion, chopped

1¾-inch piece of ginger, peeled and grated

2 cloves of garlic, crushed

1 fresh green chili, finely chopped

2 tablespoons tomato paste

1 teaspoon sugar

1¼ teaspoons salt

1 teaspoon garam masala

¼ teaspoon ground turmeric

If using dried kidney beans that you have soaked, put them into a saucepan, cover generously with cold water, and boil for 40 to 50 minutes, until tender (they should be smooth and not chalky inside). Drain, then set aside.

Put the oil into a large non-stick pan on a medium heat. Add the cinnamon stick and cumin and allow them to infuse in the oil for 3 minutes or so, then add the onion. Stir-fry the onion for 8 to 10 minutes, until soft and golden, then add the ginger, garlic, and green chili and cook for a further minute.

Next, add the tomato paste, sugar, salt, garam masala, and turmeric, and stir. Cook for another 2 minutes. Finally, add the kidney beans and ¾-1 cup of warm water, adding it little by little to create the sauce. Cook for a further 5 minutes, then take off the heat.

Serve with fresh, steaming-hot basmati rice.

JYOTI'S PEANUT SOUP
Jugu nu dal

I met Jyoti at an event to celebrate the 40th anniversary of Ugandan Asians being in Britain. She was only 13 when Idi Amin announced that he'd had a dream in which God had told him he needed to rid Uganda of all its Indians, and he gave everyone just a few months to leave before he would start to kill them. I asked Jyoti if she was scared back then. "No," she said, "at that age, I was really excited to be coming to England, but I miss Uganda now." These days, Jyoti, now in her fifties, evokes memories of her childhood by making this jugu nu dal, a beautifully humble peanut soup.

SERVES 4

11 ounces raw peanuts (sometimes sold as monkey nuts), or ready-roasted but unsalted peanuts

2 tablespoons peanut oil

2 large onions, sliced

3 medium tomatoes, roughly chopped

1¼-inch piece of ginger, peeled and grated

3 fresh green chilis, finely chopped

½ teaspoon ground turmeric

1 teaspoon ground coriander

1 teaspoon ground cumin

1 teaspoon salt (or to taste)

a small bunch of cilantro (1 ounce), chopped

Preheat the oven to 350°F.

Whether you have raw peanuts or red-skinned peanuts, it is fine to roast them just as they are (unless they are already roasted). Simply pop them on a tray in the hot oven and roast for 10 minutes. Do keep an eye on them, as roasting them for too long will cause them to burn; roast them too little and they may still be raw. The perfect roasted nut is a pale golden brown and crunchy to eat, rather than chewy. Once roasted, grind them down to a powder using a spice grinder, food processor, or a mortar and pestle.

Next, put the oil into a deep-sided pan on a medium heat and, when hot, add the onions. Cook them for 10 to 12 minutes, until golden brown. You don't want to compromise on the cooking time for the onions, as once they are caramelized they add greatly to the flavor.

Add the tomatoes and cook them until they break down and start to turn a rich red color, then add the ginger, green chilis, turmeric, ground coriander, cumin, and salt. Stir for a minute, then add the peanuts, mix thoroughly, and pour in 2 cups plus 2 tablespoons of hot water.

Boil until it thickens. Taste and adjust any seasonings. Scatter with the cilantro and serve with some basmati rice.

WILD MUSHROOM PILAU

There are over 100 edible types of mushrooms, from delicate chanterelles to fat meaty ceps, floaty oyster mushrooms to flavor-packed morels. I make the most of them by throwing them into a delicately spiced pilau, which is perfect to eat all by itself.

SERVES 4

2 cups basmati rice

10 ounces wild mushrooms, such as ceps, chanterelles, oysters, or black trumpets (or 3 ounces wild dried mushrooms, such as porcini)

10 ounces cup mushrooms

5 tablespoons canola oil

3 tablespoons unsalted butter

salt

2 teaspoons cumin seeds

1 teaspoon fennel seeds

optional: 1 bay leaf

1¾-inch cinnamon stick

2 large red onions, sliced

6 cloves of garlic, finely sliced

½ teaspoon ground black pepper

1½ teaspoons garam masala

½ teaspoon chili powder

2½ cups hot vegetable stock

1 ounce fresh dill

2 lemons, cut into wedges

Rinse the rice in at least 3 changes of water, until the water runs clear, and leave to soak in a bowl of cold water. Wipe the mushrooms clean with a damp paper towel and cut into ⅛-inch slices.

Put 1 tablespoon of oil and 1 tablespoon of butter into a large, lidded frying pan on a high heat. When the pan is hot and the butter starts to foam, add a third of the mushrooms. If you overcrowd them, they'll steam rather than brown. Leave them to cook for a minute without stirring them, then turn them over. When they're nicely browned, season and tip them onto a plate. Use the same amount of oil and butter per batch. Set aside.

Put 2 tablespoons of oil into the same pan on a medium heat. When hot, add the cumin seeds, fennel seeds, bay leaf (if using), and cinnamon stick. Stir for a minute, then add the onions. Cook for around 15 minutes, or until they are soft and have caramelized.

Next add the garlic, black pepper, garam masala, chili powder, and 1½ teaspoons of salt, and stir well. Drain the rice, add it to the pan and gently stir. Pour in the stock and bring to a boil, then cover the pan and turn the heat down to its lowest setting. If you're using dried mushrooms, rather than fresh, add them now.

Cook the rice for 20 minutes, or until tender, then add the mushrooms, folding them in gently so as not to break the rice up, and put the lid back on for a final 10 minutes.

Tear up the dill roughly and scatter over the dish. Serve with the lemon wedges to squeeze over, which will brighten all the spices.

WORKERS' CURRY
Chana masala

Right now, millions of Indians are probably tucking into a chana masala; it's the dish that sustains the nation, the coals of India's engine room. I turned many a street corner in Bombay to find a long line, eyes all trained on a giant steaming-hot wok of chana masala that was being stirred with a ladle the same size as the man wielding it. I can empathize with those waiting, as this dish is completely arresting: soft creamy chickpeas snuggled in a rich and spicy tomato sauce.

You could use canned chickpeas to make this curry, but the dried ones when cooked become so soft that I urge you to try them. Make life easy for yourself by soaking them first thing in the morning so you can have them for dinner.

SERVES 4

7 ounces dried chickpeas or 2
   14-ounce cans of chickpeas

1 teaspoon baking soda

1¼-inch piece of ginger, peeled
   and roughly chopped

2 cloves of garlic, roughly chopped

1 fresh green chili, roughly chopped

salt

3 tablespoons canola oil

2 onions, sliced

1 14-ounce can of good-quality
   plum tomatoes

1 tablespoon tomato paste

1 teaspoon garam masala

¾ teaspoon ground cumin

½ teaspoon chili powder

¼ teaspoon ground turmeric

Put the dried chickpeas into a pan, cover them with cold water, add the baking soda, and soak them for at least 6 hours. Rinse, drain, then cover with more cold water and boil for 30 to 45 minutes, until soft, discarding any scum. If you are using canned chickpeas, rinse and drain them.

Pound the ginger, garlic, and green chili together in a mortar and pestle with a pinch of salt until they turn into a paste.

Put the oil into a large frying pan on a medium heat. When it's hot, add the onions and cook for 10 to 12 minutes, or until golden brown. Don't skimp on the time, and stir frequently. When the onions have browned, add the ginger, garlic, and chili paste and stir through. Tip in the tomatoes, crushing them with your other hand before they hit the pan. Add the tomato paste, stir well, and cook for 8 to 10 minutes, or until it has become a rich, thick sauce.

Add the garam masala, 1½ teaspoons of salt, cumin, chili powder, and turmeric, and cook for a couple of minutes before adding the chickpeas. Check the consistency. I like to add around 5 or more tablespoons of water at this point, to thin the sauce a little. Stir well and cook for another 5 minutes. Taste and adjust any seasoning as you require.

Serve with chapatis (see page 196) or hot fluffy naan (see page 199).

07

SIDES

SIDES

Indians are not great at minimalism when it comes to mealtimes. Traditionally, at every meal there will be one or two main courses, a helping of rice or dal, a couple of side dishes in the form of salads, vegetables, and raitas, and then some pickles (and that's post-starter and pre-dessert). I'm all for simplicity in the kitchen, but Indian sides can really help to balance out a meal, complement a main course, or just add a little extra variety to the table.

For instance, if you're cooking something spicy, then a cooling fresh pomegranate and mint raita (see page 188) would be the perfect partner. It's not a classic Indian recipe, but one that I have created using two of my favorite invigorating ingredients.

If you're after some added freshness, then you could try making the Jaipur slaw (see page 182) – a colorful, crunchy combination of mooli, carrots, and red cabbage. Leave it long enough and it'll turn as pink as the famous Rajasthani city.

In colder weather, ferarri (see page 177) really comes into its own. A crunchy jumble of potatoes and peanuts dressed with lemon juice, green chili, and salt, it warms you up from top to bottom, just like the addictive baked masala fries (see page 176).

My favorite sidekick of all is also India's most famous salad: kachumbar (see page 185). Finely chopped tomatoes, shallots, and cilantro turn into a sort of salsa which is greater than the sum of its parts. It goes just as well with chapati chips (see page 272) for a delicious quick snack as it does with rich dishes like my creamy chicken and fig curry (see page 89), or with grilled meats like lamb raan (see page 114) or lamb kebabs with cumin and coriander (see page 109).

Finally, there are the greens. Greens which you want to eat, as opposed to the ones you felt forced to in the school cafeteria. Green beans with mustard seeds and ginger (see page 181) is one of Mum's favorite recipes. Her generation tends to eat it as a main course, but I prefer it as a side. I am also quite partial to making the spinach with black pepper, garlic, and lemon (see page 179) with almost every evening meal.

Whichever one you decide to employ as the side dish (or dishes) to your meal, you can be sure that they are all as quick to make as they are to eat.

BAKED MASALA FRIES

In this family recipe, the fries are baked but taste just like the real thing: crispy on the outside, fluffy on the inside. They're easy to make and will be gone in a flash. Date and tamarind chutney (see page 216) and ketchup go with them nicely.

SERVES 4

4 large potatoes (russets,
   Yukon Gold, or all-purpose)
2½ teaspoons salt
1 tablespoon canola oil

¾ teaspoon chili powder
2 teaspoons ground cumin

Preheat the oven to 425°F.

Peel the potatoes and chop them into your perfect fries. I cut each potato into 3 pieces lengthways and 3 again to make 9 long fat fries from each one.

Put all the potatoes into a lidded saucepan, cover generously with cold water, add 1 teaspoon of salt, and put the lid on the pan. Bring to a boil on a medium heat, then lower the heat and simmer for another 5 minutes, or until the potatoes are soft and fluffy around the edges.

Drain the potatoes in a sieve and shake them a bit to fluff up the edges, but be careful not to break them. These fluffy edges will turn into nice crispy ones later.

Put the oil into a roasting tray and put the tray into the oven for around 2 minutes to heat it. Take the tray out of the oven and carefully put the potatoes into the oil (lower them in gently so the oil doesn't splash out), then coat the potatoes with it.

Put the tray back into the oven and bake for 20 to 25 minutes, shaking it a couple of times during the cooking time to turn the fries over. When you take them out they should be crispy and brown all over. If not, leave them in for a bit longer.

In a bowl, mix together 1½ teaspoons of salt, the chili powder, and cumin, and sprinkle evenly over the fries.

Serve them as quickly as you can, while they're still hot, either by themselves or with sardines (see page 128), my spicy lamb burgers (see page 110), or lamb kebabs (see page 109).

FERRARI

Pan-fried potatoes with peanuts, black pepper, and lemon juice

"Ferar" means "to fast" by abstaining from certain foods, which a lot of Gujarati Hindus do on designated days throughout the year. Peanuts and potatoes are some of the things which can be eaten on a fast day, hence the creation of ferrari – a mix of crispy, pan-fried potatoes and crunchy peanuts dressed with black pepper, cilantro, and lemon juice (see photo on page 86).

We liked it so much that, beyond fast days, it's a dish we always used to take on picnics to the beach or to the Humber Bridge, along with Mum's family, Prince the German Shepherd, and a car trunk full of Tupperware boxes containing all sorts of other delicious things.

SERVES 4

2 ounces peanuts, unsalted and unroasted

20 peppercorns (½ a teaspoon)

3 tablespoons canola oil

½ teaspoon cumin seeds

14 ounces new potatoes, chopped
 into 1¼-inch cubes

1 fresh green chili, very finely chopped

1¾-inch piece of ginger, peeled and grated

¾ teaspoon salt

1 ounce cilantro, chopped

½ lemon

Coarsely grind the peanuts using a food processor or mortar and pestle, remove, and set to one side, then grind the peppercorns in the same way.

Put the oil into a wide-bottomed, lidded frying pan on a medium heat. When it's hot, add the ground peppercorns and cumin seeds and, a minute later, the potatoes.

Stir-fry the potatoes for around 12 minutes, until they start to brown. Spear them with a knife to see if they're done (they will slide off easily if they are), and, if so, add the green chili, ginger, and salt. Continue to cook for another 5 to 6 minutes to cook the ginger and brown the potatoes.

When the potatoes are nicely brown, check the seasoning and transfer to a serving bowl. Scatter over the peanuts, add the cilantro, and squeeze over the lemon before serving.

GOLDEN GARLIC RAITA
Lasan waru raita

The perceived wisdom in most cookbooks is that you should only fry garlic for a few seconds so that it doesn't burn. But there is a stage in cooking garlic when the white cloves, after turning translucent, start to turn golden. That's when you need to whip them off the heat as soon as possible, but also when you get a lovely deep, sweet, smoky flavor, which infuses really well into yogurt.

This isn't a family recipe, but another one born of my love for garlic. This raita takes just minutes to whip up but is tastier the longer you leave it to infuse, and it is a great sidekick to curries, especially the roasted butternut squash curry with garlic and tomatoes (see page 61), and kebabs. You can double the quantity very easily.

SERVES 2 TO 4

1 cup homemade or Greek yogurt
3 fat cloves of garlic
1 tablespoon canola oil

½ fresh red chili, seeded and finely sliced
¼ teaspoon salt
a squeeze of lemon

Spoon the yogurt into a bowl and whip lightly with a fork.

Using a sharp knife, thinly slice the garlic. Put the oil in a small frying pan on a gentle heat and, when it's hot, add the garlic. Keep stirring it around, and cook it for a minute, ensuring that it doesn't burn.

Add the chili, and as soon as the garlic starts to turn pale gold, take the pan off the heat and pour the contents, including the oil, into the yogurt and mix.

Add the salt and lemon juice and stir through. Taste and adjust the seasonings if need be.

If you're not eating it right away, put it into the fridge, where it should keep for 2 days.

SPINACH WITH BLACK PEPPER, GARLIC, AND LEMON

This lovely, fresh-tasting spinach dish goes really well with chicken, lamb, and rice. It's unlike the cooked-for-hours saag you often find in Indian restaurants. The spinach in this recipe is only just wilted, so it keeps its bright color and packs a lot of flavor (see photo on page 86).

SERVES 4

1 pound spinach
2 tablespoons unsalted butter
4 cloves of garlic, sliced
1 fresh red chili, very finely sliced

½ teaspoon salt
½ teaspoon ground black pepper
juice of ¼ to ½ lemon (depending on how sharp you like it)

Wash the spinach and set aside in a colander.

Put the butter in a large frying pan on a medium heat. When the butter starts to melt, add the garlic and red chili. Stir-fry for a couple of minutes, until the garlic starts to harden and turn pale gold in color, then add the salt and pepper and stir.

Next, add the spinach in handfuls and coat with the butter until it starts to wilt; this will take around 5 minutes. When all the spinach has wilted, squeeze over the lemon juice and take off the heat. Serve right away.

GREEN BEANS WITH MUSTARD SEEDS AND GINGER

Fansi nu saak

This old bean is one of our favorite recipes and a Gujarati classic. Mum would often cook it for dinner, but I prefer to eat it as a side. The fresh green beans are marvelous with the nutty mustard seeds, crunchy sesame seeds, and a bit of ginger.

SERVES 4

1 tablespoon canola oil

½ teaspoon mustard seeds

1 tablespoon sesame seeds

1 pound French beans, with ends removed

1¾-inch piece of ginger, peeled and grated

1 tablespoon tomato paste

¼ teaspoon ground turmeric

½ teaspoon salt

½ teaspoon ground black pepper

Put the oil into a lidded frying pan on a medium heat. When it's hot, add the mustard seeds and sesame seeds.

The mustard seeds will start to pop; as soon as they do, add the beans. Stir-fry them for a couple of minutes, then add the ginger. Stir-fry for another couple of minutes, then add the tomato paste, turmeric, salt, and black pepper.

Turn down the heat a little, cover with the lid, and cook for another 5 to 6 minutes, or until the beans are tender, then take off the heat and serve.

JAIPUR SLAW

This recipe is an update of an old Gujarati dish called "sambharo," which is a salad made from carrots and cabbage, dressed with lemon juice. My version includes some colorful friends – daikon, red onion, herbs, and a fresher lime dressing.

The red cabbage and onion have a habit of turning everything pink after a while, hence the name of this dish, Jaipur slaw, after India's famously pink city.

SERVES 4

½ red cabbage head
2 big carrots
7 ounces daikon
¼ red onion
a small bunch of mint (½ ounce)
a small bunch of cilantro (1 ounce)

For the dressing

3 tablespoons lime juice
1 fresh red chili, finely chopped
1½ teaspoons sugar
1 teaspoon salt

Remove the V-shaped core at the bottom of the cabbage. Then either turn it over and shred it finely using a sharp knife, or pop it into a food processor with the right slicer blade.

Wash and peel the carrots and cut into long, thin matchsticks, then do the same with the daikon (or put them through the food processor, too). Peel and cut the red onion lengthways and then into fine slices, and finely chop the mint and cilantro. Throw all the herbs and vegetables into a serving dish.

Put the lime juice, chili, sugar, and salt into a small bowl, and mix until the salt and sugar dissolve. Taste and adjust the seasonings as necessary – you want a good balance of sweetness, sharpness, saltiness, and heat.

Throw the dressing over the slaw just before you want to eat it, so it doesn't go soggy, then mix together and serve.

KACHUMBAR

This dish has long been a national hit in India. It combines finely chopped sweet tomatoes, cilantro, and just enough lemon juice to cut through the chopped shallots, making it a sweet and fresh addition to dinner. Kachumbar tastes better the longer the ingredients are left to get to know one another; even an hour will make a big difference.

I like to eat it with meat – lamb kebabs in particular (see page 109) – as well as sardines (see page 128) or just by itself, scooped up with a bit of bread or some chapati chips (see page 272).

SERVES 4 GENEROUSLY

1 pound good-quality, ripe baby plum tomatoes or sweet cherry tomatoes

6 shallots, peeled

2 tablespoons lemon juice

6 tablespoons olive oil or canola oil

1 teaspoon salt (or to taste)

¾ teaspoon chili flakes

a small bunch of cilantro (1 ounce), finely chopped

The key to this recipe is using the best and ripest tomatoes available and the sharpest knife you have. Wash the tomatoes and chop them into tiny cubes – ⅛-inch squares if you can. I do this by cutting the tomato lengthways, then crossways into matchsticks, and then into cubes. Put the tomatoes in a serving bowl and set aside.

Finely chop the shallots, then add them to the tomatoes along with the lemon juice, oil, salt, and chili flakes, and mix. Taste, and adjust the salt and lemon to your liking. Then cover and pop in the fridge for at least an hour.

After an hour, or just before serving, add the finely chopped cilantro and stir to mix. Kachumbar will keep in the fridge for 2 days.

Serve as a starter with hot naan (see page 199) or as part of a bigger dinner.

POMEGRANATE AND MINT RAITA
Daram anna fodino raita

Raitas are perfect for when you need something to take the edge off a spicy curry. This raita is particularly good as the juicy pomegranate seeds provide little welcome bursts of refreshment whenever you bite into them.

Amchur is a powder made from unripe green mangoes (see page 286), and in this recipe its acidity balances the sweet pomegranates perfectly. It's not essential though, so don't worry if you can't find it.

SERVES 4 TO 6

1 pomegranate

1 teaspoon cumin seeds

2 cups homemade or Greek yogurt

½ teaspoon salt

½ teaspoon sugar

3 tablespoons chopped fresh mint leaves

½ teaspoon amchur (dried mango powder)

Seeding the pomegranate is the longest step in this recipe (see page 187 for photographs). First quarter the pomegranate, break each segment in half, and ruffle out the seeds gently, using your thumbs. That way the jewels stay intact.

Once you've got your pomegranate seeds, put a frying pan on medium heat, tip the cumin seeds into the pan, and roast them for a couple of minutes. Then put them into a mortar and pestle and grind coarsely.

Spoon the yogurt into a serving dish, add the cumin seeds, salt, sugar, fresh mint, and pomegranate seeds, and mix. If you want to make the dish look pretty, you can reserve a couple of mint leaves and pomegranate seeds until the end and scatter them over the top. Sprinkle the amchur on top and serve.

ROASTED CAULIFLOWER WITH CUMIN, TURMERIC, AND LEMON *Masala phool kobi*

Cauliflower is a hero of the Indian vegetable world, but its fate doesn't just lie in an aloo gobi. Roast it with just a few spices and you'll have a vegetable you hardly recognize. At home, left to my own devices, I would eat it like this all the time. It's addictive to eat by itself but also goes really well with lamb curries, in salads, and with kebabs.

SERVES 4

1 large head of cauliflower (around 1¼ pounds)
2 teaspoons cumin seeds
1¼ teaspoons salt
1 teaspoon chili powder

½ teaspoon ground turmeric
5 tablespoons canola oil
1 lemon

Preheat the oven to 350°F. Line two oven trays with foil and bring a deep-sided pan of water to a boil.

Wash the cauliflower, pull off the leaves from around the side, and discard. Break the cauliflower into small, fairly evenly sized florets using your hands and put to one side.

Put the cauliflower into the saucepan of boiling water and blanch for 1 minute, then drain really well. Let it dry for around 5 minutes in its own steam; if it is waterlogged it won't crisp up nicely in the oven.

Using a mortar and pestle, grind the cumin along with the salt, then add the chili powder and turmeric, followed by the oil. Mix it all together really well. Lay the cauliflower out onto the trays in one layer and drizzle the spicy oil over it. Make sure the cauliflower is well coated, then put the trays in the oven for around 30 minutes, shaking them every 10 minutes or so to ensure the florets roast and brown evenly. If they start to burn, loosely cover them with foil.

Put the roasted cauliflower in a dish or bowl, and squeeze the lemon over the top before serving.

CHAAT SALAD

This salad is perfect for a long hot summer's day when you don't want to be in the kitchen for ages, but do want something fresh and full of flavor that can be made in minutes.

The inspiration for this salad was a friend's mum's kachumbar, which was far chunkier than our own, with big hunks of cucumber dotted with scallions. I've adapted it to include some pomegranate seeds, coconut, and crunchy chickpeas.

SERVES 4

½ cucumber (around 10 ounces), seeds scooped out

7 ounces radishes

4 scallions

seeds of 1 pomegranate

1 ounce cilantro

4 tablespoons canola oil

1 teaspoon mustard seeds

1 14-ounce can chickpeas

½ teapoon chili powder

¾ teaspoon salt

2 teaspoons sugar

juice of ½ lemon

2 tablespoons desiccated coconut

½ teaspoon chaat masala (see page 287)

Take your sharpest knife and chop the cucumber into small cubes (each one should be about the size of a chickpea). Chop up the radishes in the same way. Slice the scallions into thin rings and put everything into a salad bowl, along with the pomegranate seeds (see page 188 for instructions on how to seed). Finely chop the cilantro – leaves and stems – and add it to the bowl.

Next, put the oil into a small frying pan on a medium heat. When it's hot, add the mustard seeds, leave them to pop, then add the chickpeas. Fry the chickpeas for 3 to 5 minutes, until they start to crisp up nicely in the pan, then add the chili powder, salt, sugar, and lemon juice. Turn the heat down to low and add the coconut, then stir a couple of times and take off the heat.

Add the spiced chickpeas to the salad bowl and sprinkle over the chaat masala.

BREADS

08

BREADS

Indian breads are some of the quickest to make in the world. Freshly made, day in, day out, bread is part of the daily routine of the Indian kitchen.

Fresh hot chapatis are made in minutes. Naan, too, is easily cooked, charring happily on the stove. Flaky parathas, though a bit more difficult to master, are so seductive to eat by themselves, or when mopping up the sauce of a curry, they're worth persevering with.

A lesser-known rustic bread, from the fields of Gujarat, is a millet-flour flatbread which is flavored with garlic oil made from young garlic. Millet flour was the first grain to be cultivated in the world, but it's not really used very widely in Europe. This recipe (see page 203) is from my great-grandma, who was a miller of the grain.

The bread which has captured my heart, however, is the peshwari roti. While this isn't a family classic, I have succumbed to its charms over the years and created an easy version, using just a few pantry ingredients: desiccated coconut, ground almonds, raisins, and flour.

Whichever bread you choose, be prepared for the universal "law of the first" to kick in. The first one you make is never perfect and always wonky. Practice makes perfect. And it's always a good excuse to cram one down immediately.

While you don't need to make your own bread, it is simpler than you might think, cheaper, and tastier than bought breads, and more rewarding, too – so it's worth a go.

CHAPATIS

Rotli

Chapati making is a beautiful sight to behold. When the family gathers together in the kitchen, it becomes a proper little production line. With one person rolling, another at the stove cooking, and everyone else getting all floury in between, pretty soon a brilliant tower of hot chapatis starts to form to the song-like Gujarati chatter in the background.

These quick, wholesome flatbreads are the perfect sidekick to curries as well as a great wrap for leftovers. Make as many as you can.

MAKES 16 CHAPATIS (ENOUGH FOR 4 PEOPLE)

3½ cups whole grain chapati flour or 1¾ cups whole wheat and 1¾ cups all-purpose flour (plus extra to dust the dough)

½ teaspoon salt

canola oil

1¼ cups hot water

Put the flour into a bowl, add the salt, and mix together. Make a well in the middle, add 3 tablespoons of oil, and mix, using your fingers, until it resembles fine breadcrumbs. Pour in 1 cup of the water, then add the rest little by little – you may not need to add all of it – until you can knead the mixture into a soft and pliable dough, which will take around 6 to 8 minutes.

Lightly rub the dough with a teaspoon of oil (so it won't dry out) and put to one side while you get your chapati rolling station ready. You will need a clean surface or a floured board like a chapati board, ideally on one side of the stove top. You'll also need a rolling pin, a bowl of flour in which to dip the balls of chapati dough, a spatula (or chapati press), a frying pan, and a plate for your cooked chapatis.

Once all is ready, divide your dough into 16 pieces. Put the frying pan on a medium to high heat. Take one piece of dough, roll it into a ball between your palms, coat it generously with flour, flatten it into a disc, and then roll it out to around 4 inches in diameter. Lightly coat both sides in flour, roll it out to around 6 inches, and put it face side down on the hot pan.

Wait for the edges to turn white and for the chapati to start to bubble (30 to 40 seconds), then turn it over and cook the chapati for the same amount of time. Turn it over again – it should start to puff up at this point, so press it down gently with the flat side of the spatula – for around 10 seconds, then turn it over again and do the same. Check that all the dough is cooked (any uncooked spots will look dark and doughy) and put onto a plate. Cover with a towel or wrap in foil to keep warm, then repeat.

Many Indian women have mastered the art of rolling out a new chapati in exactly the time it takes to cook one, keeping a close eye on both the cooking and the rolling. It's enormously efficient and rewarding, but many burned chapatis have been sacrificed in getting there, so don't worry if it takes a while.

HOT FLAKY PARATHA
Parota

Hot flaky paratha is India's answer to puff pastry. Even the name comes from an amalgamation of the words "para," which means "layers," and "atta," which is the Hindi word for "flour."

The flatbread is first rolled into a circle, sprinkled with oil and flour to create layers, and then folded again. The end result is a really rich, flaky bread (see photo on page 200) which is a national favorite in India and popular in many parts of East Africa, too.

MAKES 10 PARATHAS (ENOUGH FOR 4 TO 6 PEOPLE)

¾ cup hand-hot water

2 cups plus 2 tablespoons chapati flour
  (plus extra to dust the dough)

canola oil

½ teaspoon salt

Before you make the dough, get your hot water ready and set it to one side (I use ½ cup boiling water and ¼ cup cold). You will also need a small bowl of flour to dust the dough with, and a small bowl of oil with a teaspoon, so that you can drizzle oil on to your paratha.

Put the chapati flour into a big bowl, add 2 tablespoons of oil and the salt, and rub through the flour until it resembles fine breadcrumbs. Make a well in the middle and pour in ⅔ cup of the water, then add the rest little by little – you may not need all of it – and knead into a nice soft dough. It should take 6 to 8 minutes.

Lightly flour a clean surface or your chapati board. Divide the dough into 10 pieces, then take one of the pieces, roll it into a ball between your palms, and flatten it. Dip the ball into the flour to generously coat it on both sides, then roll it out with a rolling pin into a small circle, 5 to 6 inches in diameter, stopping to gently dip the round in flour again if it starts to stick.

Sparingly drizzle some oil over the surface of the paratha, sprinkle it with a light dusting of flour and fold in half; this will help to create the flaky layers. Drizzle with a little more oil, sprinkle with some more flour, and fold the crescent in half again, so that you're left with a quarter of your original round.

Lightly dust both sides with flour and gently start to roll your paratha out, up and down, so that the quarter-circle shape begins to turn into an elongated triangle, like a large pizza slice.

You can start to cook this one at the same time as you're rolling the next. To cook, place a frying pan on a medium heat and, when it's hot, lay the paratha in the pan. Leave to cook for up to a minute, then turn it over and cook for another minute. Flip it over again for another 30 seconds, put half a teaspoon of oil on to the surface, using the back of a teaspoon to spread it all over, then flip it over and do the same again.

Check for any uncooked (dark) spots of dough, then take off the heat and transfer to a plate. Stack your parathas to keep them warm or wrap them in some foil. Then repeat with the rest of the dough.

AUNTY HARSHA'S NAAN

My aunty Harsha has an incredibly organized spice cupboard. All her jars are the same height, matching and forward-facing. Most wear little yellow hats and sport handwritten labels. She brings this same attention to detail to her baking, so it's no surprise that she is the best baker in the family. Her naan comes out perfectly soft and pillowy every time.

This is a recipe for a seasoned plain naan, but there's nothing to stop you from slathering it with a bit of garlic butter or topping it with anything else you fancy.

MAKES 12 NAAN (ENOUGH FOR 6 PEOPLE)

4 cups all-purpose flour (plus extra to dust the dough)

canola oil

4 tablespoons whole-milk yogurt

1 packet of dried yeast (¼ ounce)

2 teaspoons sugar

2 teaspoons salt

1 level teaspoon baking powder

1 cup whole milk, hand-hot

Put the flour into a large mixing bowl. Make a well in the middle and add 2 tablespoons of oil, the yogurt, yeast, sugar, salt, and baking powder. Mix through with your fingers until the ingredients resemble breadcrumbs, then add the warm milk, little by little, and mix again until it comes together into a dough.

Put the dough on a clean and well-floured surface. The dough will be very sticky at first, soft but fairly robust. Knead for around 5 minutes, then scrape any on your hands off using a spoon (the best way, I've found) and settle the dough by rubbing a teaspoon of oil all over it.

Transfer the dough to a bowl in which it can double in size. Cover it using a tea towel or plastic wrap, and leave it in a warm place for at least an hour. (My aunty leaves hers in the airing cupboard.)

When the dough has doubled in size, divide it into 12 pieces. Take one piece, roll it into a ball, and flatten it between your palms. Coat it in fresh flour and roll it out to around 5 x 8 inches.

Put a frying pan on a medium to high heat and, when it's hot, place the naan in it. When the naan starts to bubble – after 20 to 30 seconds – flip it over, using a spatula, and cook the other side for the same amount of time, checking regularly to ensure it doesn't burn. Flip over again and quickly press it gently all over with a chapati press or spatula, for 10 to 15 seconds. If it rises at this point, it's a bonus and means your naan will be very soft in the middle. Turn the naan over again for another 10 to 15 seconds, check that there are no uncooked doughy bits, then take off the stove.

Keep any cooked naan warm by stacking them on top of each other on a plate or wrapping them in foil, then repeat with the rest of the dough.

MILLET-FLOUR FLATBREAD WITH YOUNG GARLIC SHOOTS
Lasan na rotla

Aged 80, my grandma enjoys a bit of bingo, the occasional Bollywood film, and properly slapping a millet bread about until it's perfectly round. Her father and grandfather were grain merchants in Gujarat, which means she knows a thing or two about millet flour.

Young garlic shoots have cloves as small as pearls and resemble chives. It's not easy to get hold of them (although many Indian shops do stock them). If unavailable, you can use either wild garlic or normal garlic.

MAKES 8 FLATBREADS (ENOUGH FOR 4 TO 6 PEOPLE)

1¾ cups millet flour

1 cup all-purpose flour (plus extra to dust the dough)

¾ teaspoon salt

1 tablespoon canola oil

1¼ cups hand-hot water

For the garlic oil

4 ounces fresh young garlic shoots, bulbs, and leaves; or 4 ounces wild garlic leaves; or 6 cloves of garlic

4 tablespoons canola oil

½ teaspoon salt (or to taste)

To make the garlic oil, finely chop the garlic (very finely if you're using normal cloves of garlic) and put it into a bowl. Pour in the oil, along with the salt, and put to one side.

Put the millet flour and all-purpose flour in a bowl, mix, then add the salt and oil and rub it through, using your fingers, until the flour resembles fine breadcrumbs. Pour in 1 cup of the water, then add the rest little by little – you may not need it all – working it through the flour until you can knead the dough. Knead the dough for around 6 to 8 minutes, until it's soft and springy.

Prepare your flatbread station by lightly flouring a clean surface or large cutting board, getting a small bowl of flour ready to dip your dough balls into, and a plate for the cooked flatbreads. Divide the dough into 8 pieces. Take one piece and roll it into a ball between your palms, then flatten it and coat it in flour. Roll the dough out with a rolling pin to around 4 inches in diameter, dip it into the flour bowl on both sides to stop it sticking, then roll it out further to 6 to 7 inches in diameter.

To cook your flatbread, place a frying pan on a medium heat. When it's hot, place the bread in the pan. Once it starts to bubble, or after 20 seconds, flip it onto the other side. Cook for the same amount of time. Flip it over again and start to press all over the flatbread using a chapati press or spatula, for 10 to 15 seconds. Turn once more and press again for the same time. Check that there are no uncooked bits, which will look like darker spots of dough. When it's cooked, shuffle the flatbread onto a plate, and wrap in foil to keep warm.

To serve, stir the garlic oil up and generously spoon some onto your bread, then slice like a pizza. Eat with your hands.

QUICK PESHWARI ROTI
Peshwari rotli

I love tearing apart hot, charred bread to reveal the sweet fruit and coconut-scented steam, which inspired me to make this quick homemade version, which is essentially a stuffed chapati. You can make it in the same time it would take to order takeout, and using pantry ingredients, too.

MAKES 6 ROTIS (ENOUGH FOR 3 TO 4 PEOPLE)

For the roti

2 cups plus 2 tablespoons all-purpose flour (plus extra to dust the dough)

½ teaspoon salt

canola oil

¾ cup hand-hot water

For the filling

4 tablespoons unsalted butter

4 tablespoons desiccated coconut

2 tablespoons raisins

4 tablespoons ground almonds

2 teaspoons sugar

Put the flour into a large bowl, add the salt and 2 tablespoons of oil, and mix with your fingers until the flour resembles breadcrumbs. Make a well in the middle and add ⅔ cup of the water, then the rest little by little – you may not need it all – kneading the dough until it is soft and springy. Pat the dough with a little oil and put to one side.

To make the filling, melt the butter in a small saucepan on a low to medium heat. Add the coconut, raisins, ground almonds, and sugar, stir and taste. (You can add other sorts of chopped nuts, other dried fruit, or even grated apple, if you like.)

To make the rotis, lightly flour a clean surface and put some flour into a small bowl. Divide the dough into 6 pieces. Roll a piece between your palms to form a ball, flatten it, and coat it in the flour. Roll the dough out with a rolling pin to the size of a small saucer (around 4 inches in diameter). Dip the roti in the flour and continue rolling it out to around 8 inches in diameter.

Take a tablespoon of the filling and spread it out on one half of the roti. Fold the other half of the roti over the top of the filling so that you end up with a semicircle. Seal it by gently pressing the edges closed, working from one side to the other so as not to trap air into it.

Put a frying pan on a medium to high heat. When it's hot, throw on the first roti and leave for around 30 seconds to a minute, until the edges color and the side is browning nicely in spots. Turn it over and cook for the same length of time on the other side.

Press down on the roti with a chapati press or spatula on the back of any uncooked bits until cooked through before transferring to a plate. Repeat with the rest of the dough. To keep your roti warm while you cook the rest, make a foil nest for them to sit in.

Serve with the Howrah Express cinnamon lamb curry (see page 108) or Maharani's favorite (see page 113).

CINNAMON-LAMB STUFFED PARATHA

Kheema parota

The cinnamon-spiced lamb is a joy by itself, but in a paratha it makes for a great all-in-one snack. If you ever visit Delhi, make sure you go to the Paratha Wali Gali, a narrow street dedicated to paratha makers. It's incredible theater to watch them roll, stuff, slap, and fry dozens of these snacks in a matter of minutes.

MAKES 10 PARATHAS (ENOUGH FOR 5 PEOPLE)

3 tablespoons canola oil

1 large onion, finely diced

1 teaspoon ground cumin

1 tablespoon ground cinnamon

½ teaspoon chili powder

1 teaspoon salt

2 teaspoons tomato paste

1 pound ground lamb

For the dough

¾ cup hand-hot water

2 cups plus 2 tablespoons all-purpose flour (plus extra to dust the dough)

½ teaspoon salt

2 tablespoons canola oil

Place a large frying pan on a medium heat. When it's nice and hot, pour in the oil, add the onion, and fry for 10 to 12 minutes, until golden brown. Next add the cumin, cinnamon, chili powder, salt, and tomato paste. Stir-fry for a minute, then add the lamb, breaking it up with your wooden spoon. Cook for 15 to 20 minutes, or until there is no liquid left but the lamb is still soft, and set to one side.

To make the dough, get your hot water ready and set it to one side (I use ½ cup boiling water and ¼ cup cold). Put the flour in a big bowl, add the salt and the oil, and rub it through the flour until it resembles fine breadcrumbs. Make a well in the middle, pour in ⅔ cup of the water, then add the rest little by little – you may not need it all – and knead into a nice firm dough.

Divide the dough into 10 pieces. Lightly flour a clean surface and put some flour into a small bowl. Take a piece of dough, roll it into a ball, and flatten it between your palms. Take a tablespoon of the lamb mixture and put it into the middle of the dough. Then, using your fingers and thumbs, make a ball around the filling. Pinch it closed at the top, then roll and flatten between your palms again. Dip a piece of stuffed dough into the flour and gently roll it out with a rolling pin into a circle 5–6 inches in diameter. Sprinkle with flour to close any little holes and set aside.

To cook, place a frying pan on a medium heat and, when it's hot, add a teaspoon of oil. Lay the paratha in the pan and leave for a minute, then turn it over and cook for another minute. Flip it over again for 15 seconds, then flip it over again for another 15 seconds. Check there are no dark spots of uncooked dough, then lay onto a plate and repeat with the rest of the dough.

Eat the parathas by themselves, or with some pickle and yogurt, or salad.

PUDLAS
Gujarati chickpea pancakes

Meet India's pancake. Pudlas are made using chickpea flour and yogurt and have a lovely savory taste. It's the gold champion of a snack my mother grew up on.

You can eat them plain with just a spoonful of pickle and a lick of yogurt, or stuffed with mushrooms, lamb, scallions, tomatoes, or any savory filling you like.

MAKES 12 PUDLAS (ENOUGH FOR 4 TO 6 PEOPLE)

2 cups plus 2 tablespoons chickpea flour (besan)

⅔ cup whole-milk yogurt (plus extra to serve)

1¾ cups water

1 teaspoon salt

½ teaspoon ground turmeric

1 fresh green chili, finely chopped

4 cloves of garlic, crushed

1¾-inch piece of ginger, peeled, then finely chopped or grated

2 tablespoons chopped cilantro

½ teaspoon baking powder

unsalted butter for cooking

Put the flour into a bowl and add the yogurt. Mix together using a fork and slowly drizzle the water in, mixing all the while, to make a smooth batter with the consistency of heavy cream.

Add the salt, turmeric, green chili, garlic, ginger, cilantro, and baking powder, mix thoroughly, and set to one side.

Take a frying pan (ideally around 8 inches in diameter) and use a crumpled paper towel to rub a thin layer of butter around the pan. Then put it over a medium heat until really hot.

Spoon a small ladleful of batter (around 3 tablespoons) into the pan and tilt the pan until the batter coats the bottom of it. More often than not, pudlas don't form into nice round pancakes, so don't worry if your batter stops short of the edges of the pan.

Cook for around 30 seconds, then lift it up to see if it has browned on the underside. If so, flip the pancake over and cook for another 30 seconds before shuffling it from the pan onto a plate. Carefully rub the pan with butter again and repeat with the rest of the batter.

Serve with some yogurt on the side and some garlic pickle (see page 217), or fire-bellied garlic and chili chutney (see page 220).

CHUTNEYS

09

& PICKLES

CHUTNEYS AND PICKLES

Pickling is believed to have started in India around 4,000 years ago as a way of preserving perishable food. In many parts of India, such as Rajasthan and Gujarat, where locals rely on seasonality, pickling is still a fiercely popular activity. Many, however – myself included – just pickle for pleasure.

Both sides of my family are huge pickle fans, but it is my mother's brother and his wife who are the biggest picklers of the bunch. At my aunty Harsha's house, a large tray with copious pickles – from freshly pickled peppercorns to a fire-bellied garlic and chili chutney (see page 220) – comes out of a cupboard and lands on the table at dinner time in an almost ceremonial manner.

The origins of many of our recipes stretch back further than anyone in the family can actually remember. My grandma tells me that when she was growing up the women of the family would sit around dividing the cooking tasks between them. When it came to divvying up the jobs, her mother (my great-grandma) was always given the role of "attanu kerwanu," which loosely translates as "the pickle maker," due to her legendary pickling skills.

There are many different types of chutneys and pickles in India. Some require salting, drying, and pickling for months, and others are quick to make and fresh. In this chapter, you'll mainly find recipes for the latter – quick chutneys and pickles made in small batches so you don't need to spend hours in the kitchen or sterilize your jars. The star of these recipes is my great-grandma's mango chutney (see page 215). It's not the same as the artificially bright orange mango chutney that is often found in Indian restaurants across the land. Instead, it is made with raw mangoes and has a real bite and a good sweet and sour balance to it.

I've also included my mum's cilantro chutney (see page 212), which is a firm family favorite and which I eat by the spoonful. It goes with pretty much everything and is the perfect condiment in that it's sweet, sour, spicy, and salty in equal measure. The flavor of the cilantro is preserved and the raw peanuts add a great coarse texture, similar to that of a decent homemade pesto. You can use it as a base to create other curries (see page 99), so it's a proper all-rounder.

I always have a jar of garlic pickle (see page 217) in my fridge, as I find that its potent salty and vinegary flavors are great with dals and fish dishes. It's also brilliant at helping to spice up ham and cheese.

Of all the recipes in this chapter, the quickest and easiest by far is the lime-pickled onions (see page 221). Shockingly quick to make, this recipe produces hot-pink onions, and the helpful addition of lime reduces the dreaded onion breath (it also wins the award for Most Fun Pickle to Make).

The beauty of all these recipes is that they go with everything, from curries and naan to cheese sandwiches. Seeing their ever-increasing popularity in the UK, I can't help but feel that it's India's way of offering something back as a thank you for cricket, tea, and the railways. A fair exchange, I'd say.

CILANTRO CHUTNEY
Lilli chatni

Cilantro is to Indians what parsley is to the British. This delicate green leaf punches above its weight like a great showman and can brighten any dish with its fresh and citrusy taste. Whizzed up in this classic family recipe, it hits all the right notes. Sweet, sour, tangy, and delicious, this chutney is the perfect accompaniment to most Indian snacks.

This is a fresh chutney which is made to be consumed quickly, so there's no need to sterilize the jar to store it in. You can keep it in a clean container in the fridge for a week, use any leftovers in my cilantro chutney chicken (see page 99), or freeze it for another time.

MAKES AROUND 6 OUNCES (A MEDIUM-SIZED JAR)

4 ounces cilantro

2 ounces peanuts, unsalted and unroasted

4 tablespoons lemon juice

1 teaspoon salt

4 teaspoons brown sugar

¼ teaspoon ground turmeric

2 to 3 small fresh green chilis, roughly chopped (seeded if you prefer less heat)

To wash the cilantro, fill a bowl full of cold water and put the cilantro in it. Move the cilantro around in the water, then take it out and shake off the excess water.

Roughly chop the stems and leaves and put them in a blender. Add the peanuts, lemon juice, salt, sugar, turmeric, and 2 small chilis, and pulse them in the blender until the mixture has a smooth, almost pesto-like consistency. Add some water to help the mixture to blend if necessary. The result should be a smooth cilantro chutney which is equally sweet, fiery, and lemony. Add the remaining chili, or more lemon juice, salt, and sugar to balance it to your taste, then spoon it into your clean jar.

Top to bottom: cilantro chutney, sweet and hot tomato chutney, garlic pickle

GREAT-GRANDMA'S MANGO CHUTNEY

Keri nu attanu

This recipe was passed down from my great-grandma. My grandma tells me that ideally you must use Rajapuri mangoes when they're as "hard as cricket balls" because they keep their bite when you cook them. However, the Rajapuri mango season in India only lasts for a month from June to July, so don't fret if you can't find them. Other mangoes will work too, but try to find ones that are green, unripe, and firm, and remember to add the sugar little by little until the chutney tastes just right. It's lovely with white fish such as cod and haddock, creamy dishes, or thickly spread in a cheese sandwich.

This is a fresh chutney which will keep in the fridge for a week or so in a clean jam jar.

MAKES AROUND 14 OUNCES (A LARGE JAR)

2 unripe green mangoes

2 tablespoons oil – canola or vegetable

¼ teaspoon mustard seeds

¼ teaspoon fenugreek seeds

2 1¾-inch cinnamon sticks

6 cloves

6 black peppercorns

1 teaspoon salt

2 to 3 tablespoons sugar (reduce if using sweeter mangoes)

1 dried red chili, seeded and chopped

To chop up the mango, you'll need to cut the flesh away from the pit inside. Lay the mangoes down on their flat sides. Then turn one mango onto its narrow side and, using a sharp knife, slice the cheeks off both sides, narrowly skirting around the mango pit that lies inside.

Cross-hatch the flesh of the mango cheeks into ½-inch dice, push them outwards like a hedgehog, and slice off the cubes. Salvage any flesh from around the pit of the mango with your knife, and dice that up, too.

Put the oil into a saucepan on a medium heat. When it is nice and hot, add the mustard seeds, fenugreek seeds, cinnamon sticks, cloves, and black peppercorns and heat them for 1 minute, or until the mustard seeds start to pop.

Put the chopped mango into the pan, stir, and add the salt, sugar, and chili. Turn the heat down and cook on a gentle heat for 10 to 15 minutes.

Once it has a thick, jam-like consistency, take out the cinnamon sticks and spoon the chutney into your clean jar.

DATE AND TAMARIND CHUTNEY

Ambli kajur ni chatni

A sweet fruit (date) and a sour fruit (tamarind) combine to make the ultimate sweet and sour chutney, which is perfect to drizzle over street foods from papadum chaat (see page 43) and potato tikki (see page 46) to garlic chicken chaat (see page 93). This is a fresh chutney which will keep in a clean container in the fridge for up to a week or in the freezer for a couple of months.

MAKES AROUND 4 OUNCES (A SMALL JAR)

4 ounces dates, pitted and roughly chopped

2½ teaspoons tamarind paste

¼ teaspoon salt

½ teaspoon ground cumin

a pinch of chili powder

Throw the dates into a blender along with ⅔ cup of cold water, the tamarind paste, salt, cumin, and chili powder, and blend to the consistency of half & half.

All dates vary in their sweetness, and the Iranian dates I use are very sweet. The end result should be a balanced chutney that is sweet and sour in equal measure, but if it's too sour, add a bit of sugar, little by little. When you are happy with the taste, spoon it into a clean jar.

GARLIC PICKLE
Lasan nu attanu

When I was younger, no greater pleasure could be found than locating the final vinegary morsel in the deepest, darkest corner of a packet of salt and vinegar chips. Today I get the same flavor fix from this particular pickle (see photo on page 213). It's spicy, tangy, and mouth-watering, and it's quick to prepare. It's perfect for eating alongside curries and grilled meats and in sandwiches, too.

This chutney can be kept in the fridge in a scrupulously clean glass jar for a couple of weeks.

MAKES AROUND 8 OUNCES (A MEDIUM JAR)

1 teaspoon coriander seeds

1½ teaspoons cumin seeds

¼ teaspoon fenugreek seeds

3 whole heads of garlic

4 tablespoons peanut oil

¾ teaspoon mustard seeds

1 teaspoon salt

¼ teaspoon ground turmeric

1½ teaspoons chili powder

1¾ teaspoons sugar

juice of 2 lemons (around ¼ cup)

In a dry frying pan, toast the coriander, cumin, and fenugreek seeds for 2 to 3 minutes, until the coriander seeds are a pale golden brown. Grind the spices to a fine blend using a mortar and pestle or, better still, a spice or coffee grinder. Peel the garlic and chop all of the larger cloves so that they're the same size as the smaller ones.

Put the oil into the pan on a medium heat. When it's hot, add the mustard seeds, and when they start to pop, add the garlic, salt, and turmeric. Fry for a couple of minutes, stirring regularly, until the garlic starts to soften slightly and turn translucent. Tip in the toasted spices and the chili powder and cook for another couple of minutes. Add the sugar and lemon juice and cook for another minute, then take off the heat.

Spoon the pickle into your clean glass jar and seal with the lid. Leave to cool before refrigerating and eat within 2 weeks.

SWEET AND HOT TOMATO CHUTNEY

Tamatar nu chatni

I eat tomatoes roasted, sun-blushed, pan-fried, wood-smoked, chargrilled, and sautéed. But I love them most in a chutney. This goes very well with lamb burgers, on kebabs, and in cheese sandwiches.

This chutney is best eaten fresh, but it will keep in the fridge for up to a week in a scrupulously clean jar.

MAKES AROUND 1 POUND (A LARGE JAR)

2 tablespoons canola oil

1 fresh red chili, finely chopped (seeded if you prefer less heat)

1¼-inch piece of ginger, peeled and grated

½ teaspoon ground turmeric

1 pound ripe baby plum tomatoes or cherry tomatoes, quartered

3 tablespoons sugar

1 teaspoon salt

3 tablespoons lemon juice

Put the oil into a saucepan on medium heat. When it's hot, add the red chili, ginger, and turmeric, stir-fry for 20 seconds, then add the tomatoes, sugar, and salt.

Cook, stirring every now and then, for 20 minutes, or until it has a jam-like consistency. Finish by stirring in the lemon juice.

Spoon into your clean jar and leave to cool, then refrigerate.

MINT AND YOGURT CHUTNEY
Fodina anna dahi nu chatni

This classic cooling combination is so old, it makes the Taj Mahal look young. It tastes great on garlic chicken chaat (see page 93) and lamb kebabs (see page 109) and with pea kachori (see page 22). It's pretty versatile, so it's a good one to keep up your sleeve for when you need a quick and tasty dip. Sometimes I vary this recipe by adding a finely chopped shallot or small onion, as it makes a lovely sweet and crunchy dip for papadums and chapati chips (see page 272). If you have any left over, it makes a great addition to a sandwich or wrap alongside some chicken (especially chicken tikka).

A good tip when making this chutney is that if you're out of fresh mint but have a handy supply of mint jelly, you could use a tablespoon of that instead – but drop the sugar.

This recipe can easily be doubled or tripled, depending on what you want to use it for.

MAKES 3–4 OUNCES (A SMALL JAR)

5 tablespoons homemade or Greek yogurt
½ ounce fresh mint
1 fresh green chili, seeded and finely sliced
1 teaspoon sugar
juice of ½ lemon
a pinch of salt

Put the ingredients in a blender and whizz up to mix. Taste and adjust the seasoning and consistency, adding salt, sugar, and water as you wish.

Eat right away, or store in the fridge in a clean plastic or glass container, where it will keep for 1 to 2 days.

FIRE-BELLIED GARLIC AND CHILI CHUTNEY

Lasan nu chatni

This is an incendiary chutney that my grandma makes on a regular basis. She always wants to give me a little tub of it to take home when I visit, and I'm then left in a bit of a dilemma as to whether I should risk transporting it back on the train, lest it make itself known to my fellow passengers. It inevitably does come with me, tightly wrapped in a thousand bags and surreptitiously hidden away among my belongings.

It's often eaten with millet-flour flatbreads (see page 203) and some onions as part of a very basic meal. You need just the slightest dot of it for an intense and beautiful chili-garlic hit.

MAKES AROUND 4 OUNCES (A SMALL JAR)

1 whole head of garlic

1 teaspoon salt

1 teaspoon chili powder

1 tablespoon vegetable or canola oil

Peel the garlic cloves, then grind them with the salt using a large mortar and pestle, spice grinder, or blender. Add the chili powder and oil and stir. If need be, you can add more oil to loosen the chutney, but it should be a very thick, pillar-box-red paste.

Keep in the fridge for up to 2 weeks (away from more delicate items), or in the freezer for a couple of months.

LIME-PICKLED ONIONS
Limbu wari dungree

Something incredible happens when you add lime to onions. The acidity in the lime cuts through the onions to pickle and tame them. If you leave them for long enough, they'll all turn pink, too, brightening up any mealtime (see photo on page 23), but they work particularly well with grilled meats, like my lamb kebabs with cumin and coriander (see page 109).

SERVES 4

2 medium red onions
6 tablespoons lime juice (from around 3 limes)
1 teaspoon salt

Peel the onions, then chop them in half and slice them finely. Layer the onions in a plastic tub and add the lime juice and salt. Mix thoroughly and leave to marinate in the fridge for at least an hour.

Serve them strained of their juices and keep any leftovers in the fridge for 2 to 3 days.

DESSERTS

10

DESSERTS

Never has the gap been wider between Indian restaurant and Indian home than when it comes to dessert. The desserts presented in the UK's curry houses on those often-laminated menu cards are usually barely recognizable to the average Indian. At worst, they can feel like a list of afterthoughts: things that are easy to get out of the freezer. It's a shame, because there are more delicious Indian desserts than there are Hindu gods and, contrary to public perception, they're not all so sweet that they'll make you fear your next visit to the dentist. A brilliant dessert should bring a whole new range of sensations to your palate and counter the textures and flavors of the savory dishes that came before. For that reason, many but not all Indian desserts feature dairy. My first ever love was shrikhand, a saffron-infused sweetened thick yogurt that Mum used to keep in decent supply (see page 224). Originally made by hanging yogurt in muslin on a wall for hours to reach the right consistency, nowadays it can be ready in minutes using a good-quality Greek yogurt.

Another family favorite is fig firni (see page 226). Not only will it make your kitchen smell like sugar-spun dreams but it will (probably) change the way you think about rice pudding. It's a dish native to North India that uses warming spices and ground rather than whole rice, making it velvety smooth and perfect whatever the season.

Chocolate is by no means an Indian invention but it works wonderfully with spices, especially the ones found in chai. My weak spot for it led to the creation of the chai-spiced chocolate pudding (see page 227). It is a rich ganache of chocolate, best licked slowly from a spoon.

Spices also work wonderfully in the Sri Lankan love cake (see page 233) – something I came across on a recent trip to the area. A legacy from the Portuguese rule within the country, it combines cardamom, nutmeg, and cinnamon with rose water, honey, and lemon, creating a cake full of layered flavor combinations. It will have anyone eating it begging you to tell them what's in there. It's perfect with a cup of tea, or as a dessert with a spoonful of shrikhand.

When the season permits, we enjoy tropical fruits such as coconuts, mangoes, and passion fruits with a squeeze of lime. The first mangoes of the season lift the national mood in India like the first sunny day of the year. Keep an eye out for boxes of them in early April at your local Indian grocer's shop. If you see something of a kerfuffle going on in the shop, you'll know what it's about.

SAFFRON SHRIKHAND WITH PASSION FRUIT

Kesar nu shrikhand anna matunda

Shrikhand is an indulgent dessert, thick, rich, and on the right side of creamy without being too heavy. The longer version involves making your own yogurt and straining it in a muslin cloth the night before to remove the excess water. This smart new version uses good-quality Greek yogurt. Every yogurt is different, so if you're using a sour one you might need to add more sugar. For the best results, prepare the shrikhand an hour or so before you serve to allow the cardamom, saffron, and nutmeg to properly infuse into the yogurt.

SERVES 4

For the shrikhand

2 cups good-quality Greek yogurt, like Fage

½ teaspoon ground cardamom

¼ teaspoon ground nutmeg

6 strands saffron

5 tablespoons confectioner's sugar

For the passion fruit sauce

4 ripe passion fruit

2 to 3 teaspoons sugar

Rather joyfully, this dessert requires very little work. To make the shrikhand, spoon the yogurt into a bowl and stir in the cardamom, nutmeg, saffron, and confectioner's sugar. Mix well, then cover and place in the fridge for an hour to allow the flavors to infuse.

To make the sauce, scoop out the seeds and flesh of the passion fruit and pop them into a pan along with the sugar over a low to medium heat. Stir until all the sugar has dissolved, checking for sweetness as you go. Then drizzle over the shrikhand before serving.

BANANA PANCAKES WITH COCONUT AND JAGGERY

Gor anna dizzy nu pudla

This is an adaptation of my friend Kumari's legendary pancakes, which she serves up just next to the cow and under the mango tree in her garden in Kerala. It's a perfect combination of honeyed bananas, toasty coconut, and jaggery (an Indian sugar made from the sap of palm trees and which tastes a bit like fudge). These pancakes are great teamed with a large spoonful of cardamom shrikhand (see page 233).

SERVES 4 (1 PANCAKE EACH)

For the pancake batter

1 cup all-purpose flour

½ teaspoon ground cinnamon

a pinch of salt

2 eggs

1 cup low-fat milk

1 tablespoon canola oil for cooking the pancakes

For the filling

½ cup jaggery (or ⅓ cup brown sugar)

3 bananas (around 15 ounces), sliced into ¾-inch rounds

½ teaspoon ground cardamom (or finely ground seeds of 6 pods)

⅓ cup desiccated coconut

To make the pancake batter, put the flour, cinnamon, and salt into a bowl, and mix well. Make a well in the middle of the flour and break the eggs into it. Very slowly trickle the milk into the flour, whisking as you go, until you've used up all the milk and have a smooth batter which has the consistency of cream. Set to one side.

To make the filling, take the jaggery and bash it up either using a mortar and pestle or in a plastic bag with a rolling pin. Put it into a frying pan over a low heat, ensuring it's all in one layer. Don't stir but keep a watchful eye over it until it caramelizes, turning a lovely golden-brown color, then add the banana slices and cardamom and mix together. The bananas will release some liquid, so cook until all the liquid has evaporated, which should take 2 to 3 minutes. Then take off the heat and fold the coconut into the mixture.

To make the pancakes, take a non-stick frying pan (7–8 inches in diameter), rub the inside of it with oil using a paper towel, and get it nice and hot, then turn the heat down to medium.

Take a small ladleful of batter (or around 3 tablespoons) and place it into the pan, then quickly tilt it until the batter has coated the bottom. Cook for around 30 seconds, add a quarter of the banana mixture, and carefully spoon it over one half of the pancake. Fold the other half over the top using a spatula and press at the edges to seal. Cook for another 15 seconds on each side until golden.

Serve with a spoonful of cardamom shrikhand or a dollop of crème fraîche.

FIG FIRNI
Anjeer phirni

Firni is a fine breed of rice pudding. Like the traditional English version, it's homely, sweet, and creamy, but because firni is made with ground rice it has a rich, smooth texture. I think it's best eaten cold, with a dollop of fig jam.

The milk and rice in this recipe are both tender souls that need mothering almost constantly for 30 minutes. But the time you spend stirring firni is good thinking time, perfect for pondering on what you might do if you won the lottery or which superpower you'd like to have.

SERVES 4

For the firni

⅓ cup rice, ground

4 cups whole milk

½ teaspoon ground cardamom (or finely ground seeds from 6 pods)

5 to 6 tablespoons granulated sugar

brown sugar and ground nutmeg, to serve

For the fig jam

4 fresh figs, quartered

2 tablespoons sugar

3 tablespoons lemon juice

Be sure to have your ingredients in order and within hand's reach. You don't want to have to dash across the kitchen to dig out the spices and the sugar and leave your rice unattended.

Dissolve the ground rice in a few tablespoons of the milk and put the rest of the milk in a saucepan big enough for it to climb the sides when it boils. Stir frequently, so that it doesn't stick to the bottom. You want it to boil properly, rather than just bubble gently, which will mean paying close attention to the pan so it doesn't overflow.

When the milk boils, turn the heat right down, add the ground rice mixture and cardamom, and stir constantly. Stir, stir, stir, for around 30 minutes, until it is thicker than custard. Then add the sugar, stir to dissolve for a couple of minutes, and take it off the heat. Put it into a serving bowl, or individual glasses if you like, leave to cool, then refrigerate.

Meanwhile, make the jam. Place the figs in a small saucepan, along with the sugar and lemon juice. Cook on a low heat, stirring occasionally, for around 10 minutes, until the consistency is jam-like. Taste and adjust the sugar and lemon juice to your liking, then let cool.

To serve, take the firni out of the fridge. Add a spoonful of figgy jam on top of each portion and lightly dust with some brown sugar and then some nutmeg.

CHAI-SPICED CHOCOLATE PUDDINGS

Chai masala nu chocolate

Chocolate accommodates so many flavors, its generosity knows no bounds. In this pudding, the sweet, warming spices that work so well together in chai – ginger, cardamom, and cinnamon – combine perfectly with the chocolate to create a simple yet indulgent dessert. This recipe isn't a familiar one in Gujarati households, but it's a fantastic use of chai masala spice mix (see page 267), which every Gujarati household has. These puddings can be made a day in advance and chilled in the fridge.

SERVES 4

7 ounces good-quality dark chocolate

¾ cup heavy cream

4 teaspoons chai spice

2 tablespoons granulated sugar

a little confectioner's sugar

a cinnamon stick or some chopped nuts, to garnish

Break the chocolate into small pieces and put it into a heatproof bowl.

Pour the cream into a saucepan over a gentle heat, wait until it starts to boil, then tip it straight over the chocolate. Add the chai spice and sugar to the mixture and stir until the chocolate and sugar have dissolved.

Pour the mixture into small glasses and leave to cool, then refrigerate. Shake over a little confectioner's sugar just before serving and garnish with a cinnamon stick or some chopped nuts.

COCONUT-MILK FUDGE
Topra pak

This is a fairly ancient Gujarati sweet, traditionally made using fresh coconut and milk that has been reduced for hours. As coconut trees don't readily grow where I live now, and there's no need to spend hours reducing your own milk, we make this with desiccated coconut and condensed milk – two readily available pantry ingredients.

What's even more satisfying is that the fudge can be made within minutes (depending on your ball-rolling skills) and looks impressive, so it will stand you in good stead for last-minute dinners, bring-a-thing-to-work days, picnics, bribes, and village fète offerings.

MAKES 25 TO 30 LITTLE FUDGES

1½ cups condensed milk
2½ cups unsweetened desiccated coconut

½ teaspoon ground cardamom (or finely ground seeds from 6 pods)

Pour the condensed milk into a non-stick saucepan and put it on a gentle heat. Stir frequently so that the milk doesn't stick to the bottom. (If it does burn, the burned bits can taste quite nice, but it's a fine line between nice and horrid.)

When the milk comes to a simmer, add 2 cups of the desiccated coconut and the ground cardamom. Keep stirring over a low heat until the mixture starts to look like dough. To test whether it's ready, pinch a piece off and let it cool for a minute before you see if you can roll it into a ball. If you can, take the pan off the heat and transfer the fudge to another bowl.

While you wait for the fudge to cool enough for you to handle it, get a bowl and put the rest of the desiccated coconut into it (to roll the fudge in), and another clean plate on which to put the finished fudge.

When the fudge is cool enough to touch, roll a bit into a small ball (roughly 1¼ inches in diameter). Roll it around in the desiccated coconut and put it onto a plate. Repeat with the rest of the fudge.

You can keep these in a clean tub in the fridge for up to a week.

Tip: As a treat for my grandma (who loves a Mounds bar), we sometimes melt some good-quality chocolate and dunk the fudge into it, using a cocktail stick, then set them in the fridge until hard.

FENNEL SEED SHORTBREAD
Valiary nankatai

Sometimes fennel seeds taste like fresh toast, sometimes like nuts, and occasionally they taste aniseedy or a bit like licorice – but all of these warm flavors marry perfectly together with rich buttery shortbread. The inspiration for making this was my father. He is a big fan of eating fennel seeds after dinner in "mukwas" as a breath freshener, and his favorite cookie is shortbread.

MAKES 12 COOKIES

1½ tablespoons fennel seeds

2 cups plus 2 tablespoons all-purpose flour

1 cup plus 2 tablespoons cold unsalted butter

½ cup granulated sugar

Preheat the oven to 325°F.

Gently toast the fennel seeds in a dry frying pan over a medium heat for 1 to 2 minutes, until you can smell them. Then crush them using a mortar and pestle and set to one side.

Put the flour into a bowl, add the butter, then use your fingers to rub the butter into the flour until it resembles breadcrumbs. Tip the ground fennel seeds in and mix through.

Next, add the sugar and knead the mixture into a ball. Wrap the ball in plastic wrap and pop it in the fridge for 30 minutes to 1 hour.

When you take the dough out of the fridge it will be harder but you should still be able to work with it. Lay it on a sheet of parchment paper and lay another sheet over the top. Then, with a rolling pin, slowly and evenly roll out the dough until it's around ¾-inch thick. Transfer the dough to an oven tray and remove the top layer of parchment paper.

Bake for 40 minutes, or until the shortbread is pale gold in color (as ovens do vary). Once it is out of the oven, lightly sprinkle a handful of granulated sugar over the top and cut into fingers. I find that 3 x 1¼ inches makes for a good-sized cookie, but you may think differently. Allow to cool before eating.

LOVE CAKE WITH CARDAMOM AND POMEGRANATE SHRIKHAND

I've never had stronger feelings for any cake than for the love cake. Packed full of some of the most delicious ingredients around (cashews, honey, cinnamon, cardamom, and nutmeg), it is rich, moist, and incredibly fragrant. I like to serve this cut into small squares topped with a spoonful of cardamom shrikhand and a sprinkling of fresh pomegranate seeds.

MAKES 12 SQUARES

½ cup unsalted butter at room temperature (plus extra to line the cake pan)

1 cup sugar

6 eggs

1¾ cups fine semolina

4 ounces ground cashews (or ground almonds)

5½ tablespoons honey

2 teaspoons ground cinnamon

½ teaspoon grated nutmeg

1 teaspoon ground cardamom (or finely ground seeds from 12 pods)

2 tablespoons rose water

1 teaspoon vanilla extract

zest of 1 lemon and 1 orange

For the cardamom and pomegranate shrikhand

1 cup plus 2 tablespoons good-quality Greek yogurt, like Fage

2½ tablespoons confectioner's sugar

½ teaspoon ground cardamom (or finely ground seeds from 6 pods)

seeds of ½ pomegranate

Preheat the oven to 300°F. Line a rectangular cake pan (approx. 12 x 8 inches) with wax paper and a fine layer of butter.

Cream the butter and the sugar together in a bowl and set aside. In another bowl, beat the eggs until pale and smooth, then slowly whisk them into the sugar and butter mixture. Fold in the semolina, ground cashews, honey, cinnamon, nutmeg, cardamom, rose water, vanilla extract, and lemon and orange zest.

Fold the mixture together and spoon out into your cake pan. Place in the oven and bake for 45 minutes, or until the top is golden brown all over and firm to the touch. Leave to cool before cutting or taking out of the cake pan.

To make the cardamom and pomegranate shrikhand, mix the yogurt with the confectioner's sugar and cardamom and half of the pomegranate seeds in a bowl, then leave the ingredients to mingle for as long as possible before serving.

Serve a good-sized square of cake with a dollop of yogurt and a sprinkling of pomegranate seeds over the top.

MANGO, LIME, AND PASSION-FRUIT JELLO

Jello is my favorite dessert. Nothing beats the theater of wibble-wobbling a giant one to the dinner table to surprised and delighted family and friends. Using fresh fruit and juice makes for deliciously clean flavors, so this is perfect after a big meal, along with a little scoop of ice cream.

While the fruits are very much straight from an Indian summer, the technique for making this jello is straight out of one of my favorite cookbooks, *Jelly with Bompas & Parr*. I collect unusual jello molds for these exciting moments, but you can always use a bowl or some glasses to set yours if you don't have a mold.

SERVES 4

5 leaves of gelatin

2 cups mango juice (a carton of mango juice, or even juice drink, is perfect)

juice of 1 lime

¼ cup sugar

3 passion fruit, seeds and flesh scooped out

Soak the gelatin sheets in a bowl of cold water and leave to one side.

Pour the mango juice and lime juice into a saucepan and add the sugar and the seeds and flesh from the passion fruit. Bring the mixture to a boil, stirring every now and then.

Once boiled, turn down the heat completely. Squeeze the cold water out of the gelatin and add it to the fruit-juice mixture. Stir properly until the gelatin has completely dissolved.

Pour the jello into your mold, bowl, or glasses, and let cool before putting in the fridge to set for 2 to 3 hours.

To unmold the jello, very quickly dip it in a bowl of hot water, put a plate on top of your mold and turn it upside down onto the plate.

Serve with vanilla or cinnamon ice cream (see page 240).

Tip: If you want to add some pizzazz to your jello, you could suspend the passion-fruit seeds in it, which will look great when it comes out of the mold. You can do this by straining the jello mixture through a sieve to separate the seeds, then stirring them into the jello after it's been in the fridge for around 30 minutes.

PISTACHIO NUT BRITTLE WITH GINGER AND JAGGERY

Pista nu chikki

This is a very simple brittle which is incredibly delicious and impossible to leave alone. You can either serve it in a slab so that your guests can break off as much as they want, or if you fear they might be too conservative (or greedy), you could always make rounds.

SERVES 4 TO 6

canola oil

1 tablespoon unsalted butter

9 ounces jaggery, broken into small pieces

1¼ teaspoons ground ginger

a pinch of sea salt

¼ cup sliced or crushed pistachios

Prepare a pan by lining it with some parchment paper or foil and very lightly brushing it with some oil.

Put the butter in a separate pan on a medium to low heat. When it has melted, add the jaggery. Stir until melted, then add the ginger and salt. Stir again and cook until the jaggery caramelizes, becoming darker and thicker; this should take around 6 to 8 minutes.

You will need to work quickly now. Spread the jaggery onto the parchment paper in a ⅛-inch-thick layer, then scatter over the pistachios.

Let cool for around 30 minutes before eating. Serve alongside scoops of ice cream or as a small treat with coffee.

Ice creams, kulfis, and sorbets

Our family gets extraordinarily excited about ice cream, especially my great-aunt Lilly, who, now aged 83, grew up eating it by the seaside in Gujarat's hot summers. When it comes to ice cream, Aunt Lilly can eat most people under the table.

As soon as the sun comes out, making ice cream is our top priority. But it doesn't have to be 100 degrees outside for you to enjoy this delicious dessert, as it is fantastic at cooling the palate after a particularly fiery dinner.

The ice cream recipes in this chapter use egg yolks to make a custard before freezing it. This technique isn't common in India, but I think it gives the ice cream a pleasingly smooth consistency.

The flavors I've gone for are not particularly traditional either, but are simply born of my love for spices. You'd be surprised at how divine cinnamon, black pepper, and fennel are when infused into a sweet, cold cream. The pepper becomes earthy and warming; the fennel, light and refreshing; and the cinnamon (as always in desserts) gives a wonderful homey flavor.

If you have one, then an ice cream maker will certainly make your life easier, but it's not essential. You could hand-churn these ice creams by breaking up any ice crystals every 30 minutes or so with a whisk until the ice cream sets.

While ice creams and sorbets are very popular in Gujarat, India's original and ancient frozen delight is kulfi. I like to think of it as the Mercedes-Benz of ice creams as it is beautiful to look at, well made, and every Indian man wants one. Traditionally, you make it by reducing a large volume of milk by two-thirds and then freezing it (without churning), making it much richer and denser than your average ice cream. This can take a long time, though, so while my kulfi recipes are fairly traditional in their flavors, the method I've created, using cream and evaporated milk, means you can make kulfi in just minutes.

CINNAMON ICE CREAM
Taj ice cream

Most of what we know to be cinnamon is actually cassia bark, its cousin, which is inferior in terms of flavor and texture. Gujaratis don't tend to distinguish between the two, but since staying at a cinnamon plantation and trying real cinnamon, I can't go back. The bark of true cinnamon grows in thin, tight curls and comes only from Sri Lanka and parts of the Malabar Coast. It is sweet, woody, and spicy, and it lends itself perfectly to ice cream, giving it a warm, sweet flavor.

SERVES 6 TO 8

2–3-inch cinnamon stick
1¼ cups whole milk
1¼ cups heavy cream

5 egg yolks (freeze the whites in little bags to use for something else)
½ cup sugar

Grind the cinnamon stick in a spice grinder or with a pinch of sugar using a mortar and pestle to make around 1½ tablespoons of cinnamon powder. You can use ground cinnamon for this dish, but make sure it's fresh and still has its flavor, as old cinnamon tends to taste like sawdust.

Pour the milk into a saucepan, add the cinnamon, and heat gently until small bubbles start to appear around the rim of the milk but it is not yet boiling. Take the pan off the heat, add the cream, and leave to infuse for 15 to 20 minutes.

In a mixing bowl, whisk the egg yolks and the sugar together until pale and fluffy, then very slowly whisk them into the cream mixture. Put the pan back on a low heat, stirring constantly until the mixture looks like thin custard and coats the back of a spoon.

Pour into a bowl and leave to cool, then refrigerate for a few hours until cold. Churn in an ice cream maker until done (which should take around 20 minutes). Or pop it into a plastic box and then into the freezer, whisking it vigorously after 45 minutes to break up any ice particles. Keep whisking it every 30 minutes for 2 to 3 hours, or until frozen.

BLACK PEPPER ICE CREAM
Mari ice cream

Too often, black pepper gets pigeonholed alongside salt. Infusing it into a sweet cream will reward you with a fresh, earthy, and spicy ice cream which tastes very little like black pepper as it is used in savory food. It's unlike any other ice cream you'll taste.

SERVES 6 TO 8

1¼ cups whole milk
1½ tablespoons cracked black pepper
1¼ cups heavy cream

5 egg yolks (freeze the whites in little bags to use for something else)
½ cup sugar

Pour the milk into a saucepan, add the black pepper, and heat gently until small bubbles start to appear around the rim of the milk but it is not yet boiling. Take the pan off the heat, add the cream, and leave to infuse for 15 to 20 minutes.

In a mixing bowl, whisk the egg yolks and the sugar together until pale and fluffy, then very slowly whisk them into the cream mixture. Put the pan back on a low heat, stirring constantly until the mixture looks like thin custard and coats the back of a spoon.

Pour into a bowl and leave to cool, then push through a fine-mesh sieve or a muslin cloth to remove the pepper bits, and refrigerate for a few hours until cold. Churn in an ice cream maker until done (which should take around 20 minutes). Or pop it into a plastic box and then into the freezer, whisking it vigorously after 45 minutes to break up any ice particles. Keep whisking it every 30 minutes for 2 to 3 hours, or until frozen.

FENNEL SEED ICE CREAM
Valiary ice cream

Fennel seeds are eaten in all sorts of Indian dishes but traditionally after a meal, like mints are in England, as a tasty mouth freshener and digestive. I love their flavor, which is both sweet and warming like aniseed but refreshing at the same time, making it a perfect dessert to end a meal with. It's a firm favorite among my friends.

SERVES 6 TO 8

2 tablespoons fennel seeds
1¼ cups whole milk
a pinch of salt
1¼ cups heavy cream

5 egg yolks (freeze the whites in little bags to use for something else)
½ cup sugar

Bash the fennel seeds using a mortar and pestle. Pour the milk into a saucepan, add the fennel seeds, and salt, and heat gently until small bubbles start to appear around the rim of the milk but it is not yet boiling. Take the pan off the heat, add the cream, and leave to infuse for 15 to 20 minutes.

In a mixing bowl, whisk the egg yolks and the sugar together until pale and fluffy, then very slowly whisk them into the cream mixture. Put the pan back on a low heat, stirring constantly until the mixture looks like thin custard and coats the back of a spoon.

Pour into a bowl and leave to cool down, then push through a fine-mesh sieve or a muslin cloth to remove the fennel seed husks, and refrigerate for a couple of hours until cold. Churn in an ice cream maker until done (which should take around 20 minutes). Or pop it into a plastic box and then into the freezer, whisking it vigorously after 45 minutes to break up any ice particles. Keep whisking it every 30 minutes for 2 to 3 hours, or until frozen.

PISTACHIO AND SAFFRON KULFI

Pista kesar kulfi

The two most elegant ingredients in the Indian pantry go hand in hand in this recipe to create one of India's most famous kulfis. It's not easy to buy ground pistachios; I tend to run mine through a spice and nut grinder to create a fine powder for this kulfi. You could use a food processor to chop the nuts, but you'll end up with a chunkier nut kulfi. This scales up very well if you want to make a bigger batch.

SERVES 6 TO 8

1¼ cups evaporated milk

1¼ cups heavy cream

5 tablespoons sugar

4 ounces pistachios, finely ground

a pinch of saffron threads

chopped pistachios, to serve

Pour the evaporated milk, cream, and sugar into a saucepan and bring the mixture to a gentle boil, stirring it fairly frequently to ensure it doesn't stick to the bottom of the pan.

When it starts to boil, turn the heat down, add the ground pistachios and saffron, and simmer for around 5 minutes.

Transfer to a bowl and leave to cool down, then put in the fridge. When it is cold, pour into kulfi molds or a freezable container, cover and freeze for 2 to 3 hours.

To remove the kulfis from their molds, dip them into hot water for a second, turn them upside down over a plate, and give them a sharp tap on the top.

Serve with a sprinkling of chopped pistachios.

ALPHONSO MANGO SORBET
Haffus keri gola

Alphonso mango season was synonymous with party time as far as my grandfather was concerned. He'd head down to the wholesale fruit market to bargain for boxes for the whole family and come back with far too many. Because they're very juicy, Mum would pop my sister and me in the bath with some freshly cut mangoes, where we could feast on them with messy abandon. These days, I still buy too many, but rather than gorge myself on them in the bath, I turn them into a simple and delicious sorbet.

Although Alphonso mangoes are known for their soft, buttery flesh, they will vary depending on their quality and ripeness, so I suggest you add both the lime juice and sugar in stages, before you freeze the mixture, tasting it until you're happy with the flavor and sweetness of your sorbet.

SERVES 6 TO 8

6 ripe Alphonso mangoes
  (around 1½ pounds mango flesh)
½ cup heavy cream

juice of 2 limes
⅔ cup confectioner's sugar

To prepare the mangoes, you'll need to cut the flesh away from the large pit inside. Lay the mangoes down on their flat sides. Then turn one mango on to its narrow side and, using a sharp knife, slice the cheeks off both sides, narrowly skirting around the mango pit which lies inside. Salvage any flesh from around the pit of the mango with your knife.

Cross-hatch the flesh of the mango cheeks, push them outwards like a hedgehog and scoop off the cubes using a teaspoon. Place the flesh into a food processor or blender, and repeat with the rest of the mangoes.

Add the cream, half the lime juice, and half the sugar, and blitz together into a purée. Taste and add the rest of the lime juice and sugar as you need it.

Churn in an ice cream maker until firm (which should take around 20 minutes). Or pop it into a plastic box and then into the freezer, whisking it vigorously after 45 minutes to break up any ice particles. Keep whisking it every 30 minutes for 2 to 3 hours, or until frozen.

CARDAMOM AND ROSE WATER KULFI

Eliachi anna gulab kulfi

This was the last thing we ate at my sister's wedding, just after we had danced gift offerings (including pineapples) down the aisle to her husband's side of the family and just before my grandma started throwing some shapes on the dance floor to Panjabi MC.

Every rose water varies in strength, so it's best to add it spoon by spoon until it tastes just right to you.

SERVES 6 TO 8

12 cardamom pods
1¼ cups evaporated milk
1¼ cups heavy cream

½ cup sugar
2 tablespoons rose water

Remove the cardamom seeds from their pods and using a spice grinder, or a mortar and pestle, grind the seeds as finely as you can, then set aside.

Pour the evaporated milk, cream, sugar, and rose water into a saucepan and add the ground cardamom seeds. Bring the mixture to a gentle boil, stirring fairly frequently to ensure it doesn't stick to the bottom of the pan.

When it starts to boil, take it off the heat and transfer to a bowl to cool down, then put in the fridge. When the mixture is cold, strain out the cardamom seeds using a cheesecloth and pour the mixture into kulfi molds or a freezable container. Cover, then freeze for 2 to 3 hours.

To remove the kulfis from their molds, dip them into hot water for a second, turn them upside down over a plate and give them a sharp tap on the top.

Serve with some fresh fruit or just by itself.

DRINKS

DRINKS

The most common drink to have with Indian meals is either a glass of tap water or a glass of buttermilk or "chaas" (see page 250), made from yogurt, thinned with water, and usually seasoned with salt and crushed cumin. It might sound like an odd concoction, but it's considered uniquely perfect in India. Not only does it use up the end of the daily batch of homemade yogurt, but it spreads calm after a particularly spicy mouthful and is wonderfully restorative during the searing heat of an Indian summer.

At breakfast, when flagging, or when guests come over, masala chai is always on offer. While the English introduced tea to India, Indians drink more of it than any other country in the world and nearly always as masala chai. This sweet blend of warming spices infused into tea and milk is considered to be the sovereign pick-me-up. Ordinarily, every Indian woman's chai spice is as prized as the family jewelry collection, but my mother's recipe is in this book for you to enjoy (see page 267).

Wherever you go in India, you'll find fresh limeade and lassis, which are drunk without occasion and by the gallon every day. Saffron lassi (see page 259) is my absolute favorite – you need only a pinch of saffron to create an elegant drink – and it would be a crime not to make a mango lassi when mangoes are in season. Both can be drunk by themselves and they also go really well with street foods like kachori (see page 22), papadum chaat (see page 43), pav bhaji (see page 66) and masala fries (see page 176).

Neither I nor my family are strangers to spirits and wines, but many Indian families are. Of course you could drink beer with your meal as per the English tradition, but you needn't; the idea that Indian food and wine don't match is just a myth which needs debunking.

In our house we like bold reds with our main meals. Usually they're more fruity than tannic, especially the New World Merlots, or even a Shiraz, which often tastes a touch spicy. With dessert I like a light, honeyed Muscadet, and don't get my dad started on whisky. To help you to pick which wine to drink with your food, Sunaina, my friend and the founder and sommelier at Trishna restaurant in London, has some great words of wisdom on page 280.

BUTTERMILK
Chaas

Buttermilk is a household favorite in India because it's incredibly refreshing in unbearable heat and a great use of any leftover yogurt. The cumin seeds in this drink are loved and hated in equal amounts, so test a little out first before making the whole batch.

MAKES 2 LARGE OR 4 SMALL GLASSFULS

1¼ cups leftover yogurt
1¼ cups water
a pinch of salt

optional: ¼ teaspoon crushed cumin
    seeds, and some to serve
ice cubes

Put the yogurt, water, and salt into a large bowl or jug, along with the cumin seeds if you're using them. Whisk until frothy and well mixed.

Serve with ice cubes, and a sprinkling of cumin seeds to decorate.

FRESH LIME SODA
Limbu pani

"Can I get you a fresh lime soda, nice and sweet to beat the daily Mumbai heat?" asks the 92-year-old Mr. Kohinoor, who still waits at his restaurant, Café Britannia. There are no refusals and no regrets, either: it's a magically refreshing drink. His customers drink it under the lazy ceiling fans while rickshaws run by. I drink it at home when the summer has finally ripened, preferably in the garden and with *Test Match Special* on in the background.

TO REFRESH 4 THIRSTY PEOPLE

1 tablespoon sugar
⅓ cup water
juice of 4 limes

1 liter soda water
1 lime, quartered
ice cubes

To make the sugar syrup, add the sugar and water to a pan and bring to a rapid boil, then take off the heat. Leave on one side to cool down, then refrigerate.

Pour the lime juice in equal measures into 4 glasses. Fill up the glasses with around 1 cup of soda water and serve each with a wedge of lime and a couple of ice cubes.

Serve the lime soda alongside the cold sugar syrup, so that people can sweeten their own drinks.

GINGER CORDIAL
Adu nu syrup

Mum stands on the hearth, pointing at Dad with a rolling pin. "Can you stop drinking that from the jug? Please drink it from a glass." "But I was just cutting out the middleman," Dad replies.

This drink doesn't last long in the Sodha family, so I recommend you make enough to keep on replenishing pitchers of fresh ginger soda (see photo on preceding page) all summer long. Middlemen are optional.

MAKES AROUND 3¼ CUPS

2–3-inch piece of ginger, peeled
1½ cups lemon juice (from approx. 12 lemons)

1 cup plus 1 tablespoon water
¾ cup plus 2 tablespoons sugar

Wash your chosen bottle in hot soapy water to clean it thoroughly and let it dry.

Bash the ginger up using a mortar and pestle and set aside.

Put the lemon juice and mashed-up ginger in a saucepan, then add the water and sugar. Bring the mixture to a boil, stirring every now and then. Once boiled, turn the heat down and simmer for 10 minutes, then leave to cool for an hour.

Once cooled, strain through cheesecloth and then pour into your clean bottle.

Keep in the fridge and use just as you would any other cordial, with water, soda water, or a cheeky nip of your favorite spirit. It will keep in the fridge for at least 2 weeks.

SANJAY'S SPICED HOT CHOCOLATE

Sanjay Sharma is a man of many talents. He has six middle names, once rode around North India on a motorbike with a king cobra in a box, and also runs a tea plantation called Glenburn Tea Estate. One of his lesser-known talents (but my favorite) is making his perfect and gently spiced hot chocolate, which was served to a group of us at 2 o'clock one night in Darjeeling.

SERVES 2 TO 4

1¾ cups whole milk
⅔ cup light cream
1 bay leaf
2 cloves

1 cinnamon stick
4 ounces dark chocolate
4 teaspoons sugar (or to taste)
a few shavings of nutmeg

Pour the milk and the cream into a saucepan along with the bay leaf, cloves, and cinnamon stick, and heat until almost boiling.

Turn the heat down low and break the chocolate into the pan, stirring until melted. Add the sugar.

Remove the bay leaf, cinnamon, and cloves, and serve immediately in 2 large mugs or 4 small cups, with a shaving of nutmeg on the top of each.

INDIAN ALPHONSO

KESAR

Mangoes

કેસર કેરી
ગુજરાત કેરી

MANGO AND CARDAMOM LASSI
Keri anna elaichi nu lassi

Mum grew up in Jinja, Uganda, where the streets were lined with mango trees. She and her brothers would pick them fresh off the trees to eat before chucking the pits into a nearby ditch, only for new mango trees to appear months later.

It's much harder to get hold of good mangoes here. The season for Alphonso mangoes is short, and our supermarkets prefer selling unripe Brazilian mangoes, as they have longer seasons and are hardier. If you can't get hold of Alphonso mangoes, you can use any variety so long as they're ripe, but you'll probably need more sugar to sweeten the lassi.

SERVES 2

4 ripe mangoes (preferably
  Alphonso, Kesar, or Honey)

½ teaspoon ground cardamom (or
  finely ground seeds from 6 pods)

2 cups homemade or Greek yogurt

4 ice cubes

sugar, to sweeten

The secret to preparing a mango is to narrowly avoid the large flat pit in the middle of it to cut away the flesh. Lay the mangoes down on their flat sides. Then turn each mango on to its narrow side and, using a sharp knife, slice the cheeks off both sides, narrowly skirting around the pit. Salvage any flesh from around the pit of the mango with your knife. Cross-hatch the flesh of the mango cheeks, push them outwards like a hedgehog and scoop off the cubes using a teaspoon.

Place the mango flesh in a food processor or blender, along with the cardamom. Spoon in the yogurt, add the ice cubes, and blitz.

Sweeten with sugar to taste, and if it's a bit too thick for your liking, use a little water or milk to thin it out.

SAFFRON LASSI

Kesar lassi

I think one of the best ways to use saffron is like this, just by itself, with the yogurt as the backdrop so the saffron can take center stage. That way you get the whole caboodle of saffron's flavors coming through, from honey to Seville orange and aniseed, too.

If you make this drink the day before, it will taste much stronger and change the color of the yogurt to a beautiful sunset yellow.

MAKES AROUND 2½ CUPS OR 2 GENEROUS GLASSFULS

25 saffron threads (or a large pinch)

2 tablespoons hot water (just boiled is perfect)

2⅓ cups Greek yogurt (or homemade, but you'll need less water)

5 tablespoons confectioner's sugar

⅓ cup cold water

Take the saffron threads and put them in a small glass along with the hot water and leave to infuse for as long as you can, but at least 10 minutes.

Meanwhile, put the yogurt in a bowl and whisk in the sugar and the cold water. After the saffron has infused, whisk that in, too. Adjust the sugar or the water if you'd like to, and either serve right away or refrigerate to allow the flavors and colors to deepen.

THE PERFECT MASALA CHAI

The chai wallahs of India are soul soothers to the billion or more people who live there. Like tea lotharios, they wander the streets with a kettle of chai and a cloth bag of snacks, serenading the tired city dwellers, train travelers, and office workers with their calls for chai.

At home, my mother's chai is sovereign. Her hot sweet cups of cardamom, cinnamon, and ginger-spiced tea are the perfect pick-me-up.

Here are some tips from my mum on how to make the perfect masala chai:

1. Use the mugs you're serving it in to measure out the water and milk you need

2. The optimal chai is ¾ mug of water to ¼ mug of milk per person

3. You only need a ¼ teaspoon of chai masala spice mix per person

4. Around 2 teaspoons of sugar per person is about right to draw out the flavor of the spices

Now you know all that, you could in theory make chai for a whole busload of Indians, but here's how to make it for 2 people. For this recipe you'll need to make up Mum's chai masala (see page 267).

1½ mugs of water
½ mug of milk
2 tea bags (I prefer Yorkshire Tea)
½ teapoon chai masala
4 teaspoons sugar (or to taste)

Put the water, milk, tea bags, and chai masala into a saucepan, stir and bring to a boil.

As soon as the chai starts boiling, reduce the heat and simmer for a minute before straining through a fine-mesh sieve into 2 mugs. Stir in the sugar and serve right away.

12

HOUSEKEEPING

HOUSEKEEPING

Make your own

Day in, day out, part of the drumbeat of an Indian household is the making of yogurt, paneer, and ghee. What began as a need for self-sufficiency in every Indian house is now a ritual of daily life.

In recent times, things have changed quite a bit, with more women going out to work and storebought alternatives finally coming up to scratch, so you don't have to make your own. That being said, there's little romance in chucking a tub of yogurt into your shopping cart. It's much more fun and rewarding to open the pantry door the morning that your yogurt is finally ready, to enjoy the fruits of your labor.

Making your own stuff at home can sound drawn out, but you don't need any specialist kit or skills. Part of the reason why these things are still made at home in many households is that it is fun to do and often cheaper, too.

So if you've got time, take it and make them. You'll never be sorry you did.

Leftovers

Indians tend never to waste food. When so many people go without it on a daily basis in India, it's hard to subscribe to any other way of thinking. I've grown up with Mum transforming leftovers into a new dish for the next evening's dinner, or with eating the same dish again, which tastes even better the next day because the spices have had a chance to infuse.

Many great family dishes have been born from this way of thinking: the junglee pilau (see page 276) is one of my favorites – a bowl of fried rice incorporating whatever meat or vegetable or curry you might have lying around. Small amounts of leftover ground meat can go a long way when stuffed into a paratha (see page 206), while a bit of leftover chicken can stretch into a salad. Rice can magically turn into bread when rolled into a dough (see page 275) and old chapatis into very tasty chips in just 10 minutes (see page 272).

If you can get into thinking about leftovers as a starting point, it means you can shop smarter, too. All those odds and ends, like a bit of leftover coconut milk and a few tomatoes, could be transformed into a nourishing dal (see pages 162–7), while half a can of tomatoes could go into a basic masala to pop into the freezer for another time (see page 274).

With Indian food, all you need is a few spices (and a bit of creativity) to magic up a tasty new meal from a few leftover ingredients.

HOMEMADE PANEER

For all the subtle complexities of the hundreds of Indian spices, things are pretty simple on the cheese front. In India there is only one: paneer.

Paneer is fresh cheese, made from cow's milk and set using the acid in lemon juice or vinegar. Traditionally, it's not seasoned or flavored but is made to be used within other dishes. Homemade paneer is very different from the storebought stuff which is now readily available in many supermarkets, in that it is very creamy, fresh-tasting, and not too dissimilar to ricotta. It is also very easy to make and uses just two ingredients. You could make it early in the morning and then eat it for dinner that same day.

You'll need a fine cloth, like cheesecloth or muslin, and a heavy weight to press the paneer. I use my mortar and pestle.

½ gallon whole milk
4 tablespoons lemon juice

Put the milk in a saucepan and bring it to a boil, stirring frequently so that it doesn't stick to the bottom. When it starts to boil, turn the heat down. Add the lemon juice and stir until it curdles. You'll see the curds separate from the whey and form lumps, at which point, turn the heat off.

Line a colander with a few layers of cheesecloth and put it in the sink. Pour the curds through it slowly, draining off all the liquid into the sink. Fill the saucepan with water and pour it over the curds again to wash any lemon juice off.

Grab the corners of the cheesecloth and squeeze the water out by twisting the top of the cloth until it's tight around the ball of paneer. Keeping it twisted, put a weight on top of it to press it and leave it in the colander in the sink or set over a bowl so that any remaining water can drain out.

Leave for 3 hours or so, until firm to touch, and refrigerate until you're ready to use it. If stored tightly wrapped in plastic wrap or in an airtight container, the paneer will keep for 3 to 4 days.

HOMEMADE YOGURT
Ghar nu dahi

Rumor has it that my grandma has never bought yogurt in her life because she's made her own for the past seventy years. You don't have to make your own of course, but it's enormously satisfying to produce a rich and wobbly yogurt (not to mention delicious, easy, and cheap).

Yogurt is used in so many ways in our house: for breakfast with fruit, for thickening curries, or strained for shrikhand (a sweet, thick yogurt eaten for dessert). After you've made it once, you can keep on making a fresh batch by saving the last few spoonfuls of your first batch to use as a culture for the next one – like a sourdough starter.

You will need to find the warmest spot in the house to set your yogurt. My mum uses the airing cupboard, I use a warmed oven, and my grandma uses a shelf on top of the boiler. Most Indian families make their yogurt just before they go to bed so that it's ready to eat for breakfast the next morning. You can double this recipe perfectly.

MAKES JUST OVER 2 CUPS YOGURT

2 cups whole milk

⅓ cup whole-milk live yogurt (it's important that it contains live cultures as you need these yogurt-making bacteria)

Pour the milk into a deep-sided saucepan and bring to a boil on a gentle heat. Stir frequently, making sure the milk doesn't stick to the bottom. Once it starts to froth, take the pan off the heat and decant the milk into a bowl to cool.

According to my mum, you need to wait for it to cool down to "just warmer than room temperature" before adding the yogurt. To gauge this, stick a (very clean) finger into the bowl after 10 minutes. If the milk is too hot to keep it in for longer than a couple of seconds, it needs a bit longer to cool; if it's very warm but you're just able to keep a finger in there for around 10 seconds, it's about right. If you have a thermometer, the optimal temperature is 104–113°F. The reason why the milk has to be at the right temperature is because yogurt-making bacteria are delicate souls and the conditions need to be just right for them to thrive. If the milk is too hot, the yogurt will curdle. Too cold, and the yogurt won't set.

Whisk the yogurt into the milk so that they mix properly. Then pop a lid on the bowl, swaddle a towel around it and put it in your warm place to set for 6 to 8 hours. I preheat the oven to 250°F for 5 minutes and then turn it off and leave my yogurt there overnight. In the morning, you should have a mild, creamy yogurt.

Put it into the fridge to set. Your yogurt will last for around 4 days and, as with most live yogurts, it will become a bit more flavorful and tart with time. Don't forget to leave a little aside (around ⅓ cup) to use as a culture to make your next batch. Just add it at the same stage you would add the live yogurt in the recipe.

CHAI MASALA SPICE MIX

Chai nu masalo

Chai is India's most popular drink, and everyone, from maharajas to street dwellers, drinks it daily. This is my mother's recipe, which I use every day in my masala chai (see page 260). In our family we love the taste of ginger, cinnamon, and cloves, so our chai masala contains more of those than the other spices, pepper and cardamom.

If you have trouble finding your own ground cardamom or cloves locally, you can make your own in a clean coffee grinder or buy them online.

4 tablespoons ground ginger

2 tablespoons ground cinnamon

2 tablespoons ground cloves

1 tablespoon ground black pepper

1 tablespoon ground cardamom

Put the spices in a jar, screwing the lid on very tightly before shaking vigorously to mix them. To store, keep the jar out of direct sunlight, and use within 6 months.

MUM'S GARAM MASALA

"Garam masala" literally means "hot mix," but hot refers to the warming characteristics of each of the spices rather than to how spicy they are. Putting together a blend of garam masala is akin to creating the perfect football team: you pick your best players. Mum's favorite picks, in order, are cinnamon, black pepper, cloves, ginger, and cardamom.

Garam masala tastes great when used in meat dishes like Mum's chicken curry (see page 100), but it's also wondrous in the workers' curry (see page 173).

Ideally, you need a spice grinder to make this, but you can use freshly bought ground spices as the next best alternative (see Recommended suppliers, page 309).

1 ounce cinnamon sticks (10 approximately 3-inch sticks)

1 tablespoon black peppercorns

1 tablespoon cloves

1 teaspoon ground ginger

1 teaspoon cardamom seeds (podded)

Put a small frying pan on a medium heat and, when it's hot, roast the cinnamon sticks, peppercorns, and cloves for 1 minute, swirling the spices around the pan to roast them evenly. Tip them into a spice grinder, and add the ground ginger and cardamom seeds (neither of which need roasting). Blitz to a fine powder and keep in an airtight container or a glass jar for up to 3 months.

HOMEMADE GHEE

The smell of ghee is intoxicating and homey, like the smell of toasted nuts. It's the smell that unites every Indian kitchen the world over. It's made by heating butter gently on a low heat until the whey separates from the milk solids to leave a clarified butter, ghee. You can use it to cook with as it is very stable at a high heat, but because it is such a pure (but delicious) fat, I use it sparingly, mostly to enrich a dish at the end of cooking. If it's cold outside, a little bit spread on chapatis or stirred into rice doesn't go amiss. It's always good in my mum's chicken curry (see page 173).

A secret joy which comes with making your own ghee is the cook's spoils at the end: the bits left at the bottom of the pan are delicious and worth elbowing others out of the way for. Best eaten with a bit of bread.

1 cup salted or unsalted butter

Put a saucepan on a low heat and pop the butter in it. Leave it to melt slowly and then cook for around 20 minutes, without touching it. It's important not to stir the butter because you need the ghee to form while the milk solids fall to the bottom of the pan.

During the process, a white film will form on top and milky bubbles will push through to the surface. When the bubbles forming at the top are crispy and clear (and no longer milky), your ghee is ready.

Take the pan off the heat and let it cool down for around 20 minutes, then delicately move the film off the top using a spoon or spatula and discard. Pour the clear liquid into a jar through a sieve, leaving the milk solids behind at the bottom of the pan (to nibble on at the end).

Your ghee should keep for a month or two either in the fridge or in a cupboard, because all the elements which could spoil will have been cooked out.

TOASTED PAPADUMS
Papad

You might have been living under false pretenses that we Indians eat papadums as a starter, but it's not true. We actually eat them alongside a meal to add texture and variety.

Packets of raw papadums are available fairly cheaply online and in Indian supermarkets; they might also be called "papads" and are traditionally made with urad flour, from ground matpe beans. I much prefer the flavor of papadums I have toasted myself to the ones you find in curry houses, which are very subtle and mostly just carriers of sweet chutney.

There is more than one way to cook a papadum. You can deep-fry it, grill it, or roast it on an open fire, but I prefer to toast mine in a dry pan for speed, taste, and an oil-free finish. Each papadum will only take around 30 seconds to cook.

a packet of plain, uncooked papadums

Heat a non-stick frying pan until very hot (it should be hard to put the flat of your hand close to the top of the pan). With a pair of tongs at the ready, put the papadum onto the pan. The papadum should start to bubble and curl right away. Smooth down the curling sides with the tongs, and after 15 seconds turn the papadum over and cook it for another 15 seconds. Dark brown spots are completely normal when cooking it this way. When it is done, take it off the heat.

Before starting the next one, wait for it to cool and take a bite. It should be very crisp. If it's still chewy, try turning the heat up before cooking the next one, or cook it for a little longer.

Serve your papadums with mango chutney (see page 215), and mint and yoghurt chutney (see page 219) – but add a small, very finely diced onion to give a bit of sweetness and crunch.

To make a papadum bowl

These edible bowls are a great way to serve food, like the roasted aloo gobi salad on page 74. They're really quick and easy, too.

First get one small bowl and one slightly bigger one, and turn them both upside down on your work surface. Using some tongs, take a hot and freshly cooked papadum (which will still be soft) and place it over the bottom of the small bowl, then sandwich it with the bigger bowl. Leave it for up to 10 seconds to form the shape before removing.

Keep your papadum bowls somewhere dry, and eat them on the day you make them as they tend to lose their crunch the following day.

SPROUTED BEANS
Funguyela mug

For me, the idea of growing your own meal is really exciting, especially if it only takes a couple of days before you can eat the rewards. Without too much provocation, these little pantry legumes easily turn from mung beans into fresh, crunchy, and nutritious sprouts.

I normally start my beans first thing in the morning, and they will take 48 to 72 hours to sprout. They are fantastic thrown into salads (see papadum chaat, page 43) and dressed in garlic, lemon juice, and cumin (see page 83) – one of my favorite ever dishes.

7 ounces mung beans (will produce
   around 1¼ pounds beans)

Give the mung beans a good rinse in cold water, drain them, then put them on a flat-bottomed, high-sided dish. Cover them with about an inch of hand-hot water, put a plate or some plastic wrap over the top of them (but poke a few holes in the top of the wrap), and leave them somewhere warm for 24 hours. A warm cupboard is perfect.

The next day, drain the beans and rinse them. You may have a few small sprouts growing. Again, add about an inch of hand-hot water to the bottom of the dish. Cover and leave for another 24 hours in the same warm place.

The next day, you should have some lovely crisp white sprouts. Rinse them one final time and drain.

If your beans have not sprouted, it could be that they need somewhere a bit warmer and a little more time. Rinse them and put paper towels on the bottom of the dish to help distribute the heat evenly, then put the beans on the paper towels and add a bare minimum of hand-hot water, around ⅛ inch, to the bottom of the dish (you need to keep the sprouts relatively dry as otherwise they might rot). Leave them somewhere warmer for another 12 to 24 hours, then rinse and drain.

If you're not using them right away, leave them to dry out before storing in a clean tub in the fridge until needed. Eat within 2 to 3 days.

CHAPATI CHIPS

Unless it's the middle of winter and the birds are looking hungry, we tend to turn old chapatis into these chips. Chapatis crisp up nicely in the oven in only 10 minutes and these are great eaten just by themselves, sneaked into salads, or loaded with kachumbar (see page 185), cilantro chutney (see page 212), or any other dip you fancy.

SERVES 4

6 to 8 chapatis
canola oil, for drizzling
a pinch of salt
½ teaspoon chili powder
optional: a pinch of chaat masala (see page 287)

Preheat your oven to 350°F.

Cut your chapatis into triangles, like small pizza slices, and pop them on a baking tray. Drizzle with oil and sprinkle with the salt and chili powder. Put them in the oven and bake for around 10 minutes, or until crispy.

Sprinkle with the chaat masala, if using, and serve.

BASIC TOMATO MASALA
Tametar nu masala

You can use this tomato masala as the base for a new curry if you happen to have some canned tomatoes left over. You can easily freeze it and then defrost it before cooking. The quantities given here can be doubled or tripled, which will make quick work of many of the tomato-based curries in this book. When you defrost the masala, you'll just need to add salt and spices according to the recipe you're using.

MAKES ENOUGH MASALA FOR 1 CURRY (SERVING 4)

2 tablespoons canola oil
1 onion, chopped
1¼-inch piece of ginger, peeled
2 to 3 cloves of garlic, crushed

1 fresh green chili or 1 fresh red chili or ½ teaspoon chili powder
7 ounces canned tomatoes (½ a can)
1 tablespoon tomato paste

Put the oil into a lidded frying pan on a medium heat. When the oil is hot, add the onion and fry for 6 to 8 minutes, until soft and starting to turn golden. Add the ginger, garlic, and chili and fry for 3 to 4 minutes, stirring occasionally.

Tip in the canned tomatoes, pouring them into the pan with one hand and crushing them with the other (if the tomatoes are whole) before they hit the pan, and add the tomato paste. Pop the lid on, turn the heat down to low, and cook for 8 to 10 minutes, stirring occasionally, until the tomatoes break down and turn a nice dark red with a paste-like consistency.

Leave to cool before storing in the freezer in a tight Tupperware box or as individual portions in freezer bags.

LEFTOVER RICE FLATBREAD
Bhat wara thepla

This is such a delicious flatbread that I would suggest cooking extra rice just so you can make it. As with eating any leftover rice, the golden rule is that if it's been kept in the fridge, it's fine for up to 2 days.

MAKES 10 FLATBREADS

1¼ cups cooked rice

1 cup chapati flour (plus extra to dust the dough)

½ cup chickpea flour (besan)

optional: 1½ tablespoons sesame seeds

1 teaspoon cumin seeds, bashed a little

1 teaspoon salt

¾ teaspoon chili powder

¾ teaspoon ground turmeric

1 teaspoon sugar

canola oil

½ cup hand-hot water

Put the rice into a bowl and break up any clumps using your hands. Add the flours, the sesame seeds if using, the cumin, salt, chili powder, turmeric, and sugar, and mix together. Make a well in the flour mixture and add 2½ tablespoons of oil, then mix, and start to add the water, kneading it through. You want enough water for a soft texture which will be very slightly sticky. If it's too tough, add a little more.

Rub a teaspoon of oil on your hands and over the dough. You don't need to let the dough rest, so simply divide it into 10 pieces the size of golf balls – don't worry if they're a little sticky.

Get your rolling station ready. You'll need a rolling pin, a lightly floured surface or board, like a chapati board, and a small bowl of chapati flour to dust the dough. Roll a piece of dough into a ball between your palms, flatten it, then dip it into the flour, and lay it on your board.

Roll it into a circle about 4 inches in diameter with a rolling pin, and dip it into the bowl of flour if need be. Then roll it out to a circle about 6 inches in diameter.

Place a frying pan on a medium heat and, when it's hot, lay the flatbread in it. Cook for about 20 seconds (or until the edges brown), then flip it over using a spatula and add ¼ teaspoon of oil on the cooked side. Leave for another 20 seconds, flip it over and add a little more oil. Flip it again and press it down with a spatula or the back of a large spoon. Check there are no uncooked dark doughy bits, then transfer to a plate and cover with a clean tea towel to keep warm.

If it is your first attempt, now is about the time you might be wishing you'd bought your flatbreads and given the rice to the birds, but I promise you this gets much easier with a little practice. Continue with the rest of the dough until you have a lovely plate of fresh flatbreads.

JUNGLEE PILAU
Indian fried rice

Leftover rice is one of the easiest things to breathe new life into, using just a few ingredients. If you don't have everything on the ingredients list, chuck in what you do have, like any leftover vegetables hanging around at the bottom of the fridge or meat from last night's curry.

As with eating any leftover rice, make sure it's been kept in the fridge and for no longer than 2 days.

SERVES 4

3 tablespoons canola oil

1 medium onion, chopped

3 cloves of garlic, roughly chopped

½ teaspoon cumin seeds

1 teaspoon ground turmeric

½ teaspoon chili powder

optional: around 1 cup cooked meat, vegetables or leftover curry

¾ cup plus 2 tablespoons green peas

3½ cups leftover cooked rice

1¼ teaspoons salt (but take it easy on the salt if you previously salted the rice)

4 scallions, finely sliced

a squeeze of lemon, to serve

Put the oil into a wide-bottomed, lidded frying pan on a medium heat. When the oil is hot, add the onion and fry for 10 to 12 minutes, until golden brown, then add the garlic, and cumin seeds, turmeric, and chili powder and stir to mix.

Transfer your meat, vegetables, or leftover curry to the pan, stir, and cover with the lid. Leave to heat through for around 5 or 6 minutes, then add the peas and rice. Stir again gently so as not to break up the rice grains too much, and cover with the lid. Cook for 6 to 8 minutes, or until the rice is properly heated through and steaming.

Season the rice with the salt, sprinkle over the chopped scallions, and serve with a generous squeeze of lemon.

What to do with leftover . . .

Chapatis
Turn them into chips (see page 272), chapati wraps (see page 64), or feed them to the birds.

Chickpeas
Roast them up into some spicy snacks like my chana ka chips (see page 40).

Coconut milk
Throw it into the daily dal (see page 166) or make the 100 garlic-clove curry (see page 62).

Eggs
Make some inda boflo – Ugandan eggy bread (see page 147).

Meat curries or ground meat, roast or grilled meat
Add any leftover meat curries to rice such as the junglee pilau (see page 276), or the cinnamon and clove pilau with cashew nuts (see page 156).

Try stuffing ground meat into the cinnamon-lamb stuffed paratha (see page 206) or add it to the eggplant and cherry tomato curry (see page 57).

Swap the mushrooms for roast or grilled meat in the wild mushroom pilau (see page 170), or substitute the paneer for meat in the chapati wraps with spicy vegetables (see page 64). You can also eat your meat with a chaat salad (see page 192) and some mint and yogurt chutney (page 219).

Rice
Make some lovely junglee pilau (see page 276) or turn it into some tasty flatbread (see page 275).

Canned tomatoes
Turn them into a tomato masala (see page 274), which you can use as the base for any curry.

Vegetables and vegetable curries
Transform potatoes into the belly-warming bateta nu shaak (see page 63).

Add any vegetable curry to the cinnamon and clove pilau with cashew nuts (see page 156).

Turn any odd vegetables you have lingering around into Mumbai's most popular leftover dish, pav bhaji (see page 66).

Menu ideas

The way we eat at home as a family has changed wildly over the years. The women of my grandma's generation stayed at home to look after the household and make the family meals, which were elaborate feasts. Women of my generation work, and we've adopted local ingredients and modernized techniques, and like to mix and match according to mood and season. All those changes are reflected in the suggested menus below, but I've included a traditional Gujarati menu just out of interest.

There are two types of cooking: everyday and for an event. At home, during the week, I'll cook one main dish, which I'll serve sometimes with leftovers (Indian leftovers are always delicious the following day), with either chapatis or rice, along with yogurt and a pickle from the fridge.

When it comes to having friends or family over, I tend to make a few courses, but nothing too formal: it's a free-flowing affair, with big sharing bowls and dishes in the middle of the table for people to help themselves, and a stack of chapatis on the side. Below are a few sample menus which suit both types of cooking, but feel free to mix and match. For me, the perfect menu is all about balance, so I like to make sure there's a good range of flavors, textures, and spices.

For 2 meat eaters

Pan-fried chicken livers in cumin butter masala

Salmon and spinach curry *with* rice *or* chapatis

Fennel seed ice cream

* * *

Fire-smoked eggplants *with* chapati chips

Mum's chicken curry *with* spinach with black pepper, garlic, and lemon *and* rice

Saffron shrikhand with passion fruit

For 2 vegetarians

Fire-smoked eggplants *with* chapati chips

Fresh spinach and paneer *with* chapatis

Cinnamon ice cream

* * *

Chili paneer

Wild mushroom pilau *with* chaat salad

Chai-spiced chocolate puddings

For 4 meat eaters

Beet and feta samosas *with* cilantro chutney

Coconut fish curry *with* rice *and* green beans with mustard seeds and ginger

Black pepper ice cream

* * *

Chili paneer

Whole roast masala chicken *with* ferrari *and* spinach with black pepper, garlic, and lemon

Cinnamon ice cream *with* fennel seed shortbread

For 4 vegetarians

Corn on the cob with chili garlic butter

Roasted butternut squash curry with garlic and tomatoes *with* chapatis *and* green beans with mustard seeds and ginger

Love cake with cardamom and pomegranate shrikhand

* * *

Papadum chaat

Dal makhani *with* parathas *and* spinach with black pepper, garlic, and lemon

Sanjay's spiced hot chocolate *with* pistachio-nut brittle with ginger and jaggery

For 6 meat eaters

Chicken and coriander samosas *with* cilantro chutney

Slow-cooked lamb and spinach curry *with* golden garlic raita *and* rice *or* naan

Love cake with cardamom and pomegranate shrikhand

* * *

Royal Bengal fish fingers *with* sweet and hot tomato chutney

Lamb kebabs with cumin and coriander *with* kachumbar *and* pomegranate and mint raita *and* naan

Chai-spiced chocolate puddings

For 6 vegetarians

Beet and feta samosas *with* cilantro chutney

Workers' curry *with* eggplant and cherry tomato curry *and* parathas

Cinnamon ice cream *with* fennel seed shortbread

* * *

Pea kachori *with* lime-pickled onions *and* mint and yogurt chutney

Fresh spinach and paneer *and* daily dal *with* rice *and* chapatis

Pistachio and saffron kulfi

For 8 meat eaters

Corn on the cob with chili garlic butter

Spicy lamb burgers *with* Jaipur slaw *and* sweet and hot tomato chutney *and* baked masala fries

Cardamom and rose water kulfi

* * *

Papadum chaat

Maharani's favorite *with* chapatis *and* Jaipur slaw *and* pomegranate and mint raita

Fig firni

For 8 vegetarians

Pea kachori *with* lime-pickled onions *and* mint and yogurt chutney

Slow-cooked red pepper and paneer curry *with* chana dal with golden garlic tarka *and* spinach with black pepper, garlic, and lemon *and* parathas

Cardamom and rose water kulfi

* * *

Beet and feta samosas *with* cilantro chutney

Roasted butternut squash curry with garlic and tomatoes *with* cauliflower, cashew, pea, and coconut curry *and* rice *and* naan

Love cake with cardamom and pomegranate shrikhand

A traditional Gujarati menu from my grandma's generation

Farsan (snacks), as a starter:

Samosas *or*

Kachori *or*

Dhokla *or* bhajia (onion or vegetable bhajis) *with*

Cilantro chutney

A thali for main course:

Two or three vegetable dishes such as bateta nu shaak, okra, eggplant *with*

Toor dal *and*

Kitchari *or*

Jeera rice

Other accompaniments

Chapatis

Kachumbar

Papadums

Cilantro chutney

Yogurt

Lasan nu chatni

To drink

Buttermilk

Fresh lime soda

To finish

Shrikhand

WINE AND INDIAN FOOD
by Sunaina Sethi

Drinking wine with Indian food is often scoffed at, but creamy lassis and chilled lagers are not the only things that can hold their own against the complexity and richness of an Indian feast.

There are, of course, no fixed rules as to what specific wines to drink with Indian dishes. Matching food and wine is a highly subjective area, so here are a few pointers and principles when picking a match.

The same general rules apply to Indian food as to all food: white wine for fish and white meat such as chicken, turkey, and pork, and red wine for red meat such as lamb and game. However, the cooking methods and spices used in Indian food can take you happily in another direction, too: a red wine with a white meat dish, for instance. Tandoori dishes, which have a smoky flavor, should not be matched with red wines which are particularly tannic, however, as this can cause an unpleasant aftertaste.

On the other hand, aromatic grape varieties such as Albariño, Riesling, Viognier, and Gewürztraminer are wonderful paired with many Indian dishes, as their aromas tend to complement the saffron, nutmeg, cinnamon, and cardamom which often form the bedrock of Indian dishes. Similarly, food with an extra kick can often benefit from being matched with wines with a higher sugar content.

Street food

Street food such as chaats and aloo tikkis have many complex flavors going on. Street food is salty, sweet, tangy, and spicy, all at the same time, so it is important to find a wine that complements all these elements without overpowering any of them or getting lost amidst the flavors.

The first option for me would be an aromatic wine, such as a Riesling or Pinot gris from Alsace, which will have a touch of residual sugar to mellow the spiciness and allow the fragrances to bounce off each other playfully. Alternatively, a medium-bodied red wine, such as an Austrian Zweigelt, which showcases some bold red fruit like cherries and plums, can be a great option.

Vegetarian

Dal makhani (see page 167) has a fantastic richness to it. Something with a good balance of acidity and fruit will match nicely, such as a young red wine from Rioja. A lighter style of dal, such as the chana dal with golden garlic tarka (see page 162), could be matched with a Fiano from the region of Campania in southern Italy, which has spicy honey flavors, or even one of my personal favorites, a Malvasia from Istria, aged in acacia wood.

Paneer

Paneer dishes can often be matched with a Chardonnay from Burgundy, which has a hint of oak. For those more adventurous, an aged Savennières from the Loire Valley makes for a very interesting match with paneer due to its slightly oxidized style.

Tomato and garlic

Dishes with a lot of tomatoes and garlic, like the tomato fry (see page 77), scream out for a Puglian red wine such as Primitivo, or perhaps a Valpolicella Ripasso.

Rice

Rice dishes also play an important part in Indian cuisine, and they should not be missed when considering the wine. Delicate rice dishes, like wild mushroom pilau (see page 170), can be matched with some of the aromatic wines – Albariño in particular, or a rosé from Provence – or even perhaps a Pinot noir from Martinborough in New Zealand, which will also bring out the best of the flavors in a biryani or pilau.

Fish

Mustard seeds are often used in Indian cuisine, especially with seafood, like the jumbo shrimp with garlic and mustard seeds (see page 138). A lightly oaked Chardonnay will complement the flavor of dishes like this well.

With a coconut fish curry (see page 127), a dry, limey Australian Riesling will provide the required acidity for the creaminess of the curry as well as for the oiliness of the fish. Where a slightly meatier fish is used, such as monkfish, a red wine, such as an Austrian Zweigelt, would also work well.

Meat

Creamy chicken curries are best matched with either a New World Riesling or a Soave from Veneto. These have enough acidity to lift the creaminess of the dishes, and also some good fruit behind them to stand up to the flavors.

Bold lamb curries and lamb raan (see page 114) will take many varieties, but you must consider the alcohol levels of the wine, as these can sometimes intensify the spices, causing them to become overpowering. Personally, I think Spanish wines, especially from Ribera del Duero, Priorat, and Montsant, are very well suited as they have an intense fruit concentration and a well-integrated oakiness that perfectly complement the cinnamon and cumin so often found in these dishes.

Desserts

Indian desserts often incorporate spices such as cardamom and cinnamon, as well as rose water. They are frequently rich and sweet, so the dessert wine you drink with them must be sweet (or even sweeter!), with a lot of acidity, to lift the dessert. A sweet Gewürztraminer complements all these flavors, as will a young Riesling.

With even richer desserts involving fudge, chocolate, and jaggery, try a Red Muscadelle, which will complement deeper, toasty flavors.

Finally, my advice is to be adventurous and keep tasting!

Sunaina Sethi is a friend, founder, and sommelier at the Michelin-starred restaurant Trishna in London.

How to eat with your hands

It's strange to see how intimidated people are by the idea of eating food without cutlery when you have two perfectly formed utensils: your hands. Putting hand to food to mouth is much more fun than scraping your food off a steel prod, and it gives you a much greater connection to what you're eating and a lovely sense of communion around the table. We Sodhas still eat using our hands at home.

It's traditional to eat with your right hand, unless you're left-handed, like me. Tear a bit of chapati off with this hand, using your thumb and fingers.

If eating a meat curry or substantial vegetable curry, hold the piece of bread around the edges using your fingertips, and cover a piece of meat or vegetable. Clamp your fingers together over it, like a toy claw machine or a crane, and aim for your mouth.

If eating a dal or a dish with a bit more sauce, like a chickpea curry, you can pinch your piece of bread at one end and in the middle to form a scoop.

Help

Sometimes you can rescue a dish; sometimes it's best to have a local pizza delivery number on hand. If you find yourself with one of the problems below, here are some suggestions for what to do.

What's your problem?

Too much chili

Unfortunately chili is a blunt instrument and it isn't forgiving when you use too much. If the curry is tomato-based, you could add a can of tomatoes (removing any meat first if already cooked), then cook it for another 20 minutes or so, before returning the meat. Or try doubling the volume of the other ingredients (except the chili, of course). Alternatively, try adding a tablespoonful of whole yogurt or some coconut milk to your meal, depending on the type of curry, which occasionally works to take the edge off.

Too much salt

Overenthusiastic salting isn't necessarily a disaster. There's an old wives' tale that says you should add half a raw potato to soak up the additional salt, but I think adding more ingredients, building around the salt, is a better way of diluting it. Try adding more meat or vegetables or doubling the quantity of all the other ingredients except the salt.

Not saucy enough

This isn't that kind of book, I'm afraid. But if you're looking for a bit of extra sauce in your dish or curry, be sure to cook it well, then try adding a small amount of warm water a splash at a time, until you have as much as you would like. If you've altered the consistency by a fair bit, be sure to taste and adjust the salt or spice as required. Alternatives to water are whole yogurt, light cream, or tomatoes (but be sure to give the tomatoes extra time to cook through).

My chapatis are not soft enough

Flours tend to vary, which means breads will vary, too. Softness is the result of a few different things: oil, water, and the temperature you cook at.

If your dough is too robust, try poking holes in it using your finger and adding a small amount (1 to 2 tablespoons) of hot water. Leave to soak for a few minutes and knead until mixed. Then try cooking again on a higher temperature but for a shorter period of time to see if that makes a difference.

Too much rose water

Less is best when it comes to rose water, as too much can overpower a dish. If you have put too much into a kulfi (see page 247), try to increase the quantities of cream and evaporated milk, adjusting the sugar as well until it tastes just right.

If you have put too much into a curry, try to level it out by adding more ingredients such as lemon juice or cream.

Too much lemon juice

Lemons can sometimes be a bit unpredictable. Use too much lemon juice and you'll need something to take the edge off the tartness. Depending on the dish, you could try adding a little sugar (start with ½ teaspoon) to balance it out, or a little cream.

Too watery

Try spooning out excess water or taking out any ingredient that would suffer from additional cooking, like meat, fish, or veg, and reducing the liquid in an uncovered pan on a medium heat.

Other Indian cooking problems

Garlic-smelling hands

As much as I love garlic, I'm not a big fan of the smell that raw garlic can leave on your hands. Try rubbing them on a stainless-steel pan, utensil, or the sink. This sounds a bit odd, but it does work. Alternatively, you can rub your hands with baking soda and wash it off.

Turmeric stains

Turmeric will indiscriminately stain everything you let it near, and it is tough to get out. To remove stains on your hands and nails, a bit of fairly vigorous scrubbing with soap and a nail brush tends to do the trick.

To remove stains from your clothes, take action fast and soak them in detergent or baking soda and water. Then wash using a stain remover.

To avoid a turmeric-stained table, I use some bright yellow place mats, but if it manages to get on to wood, try scrubbing with a combination of lemon juice and soap.

Indian ingredients

Spices

To the uninitiated, spice racks can be intimidating. Strange seeds, dusty barks, and weird-looking powders; all sorts of colors, textures, and shapes, crammed into a hodgepodge of jars, with no helpful explanations attached.

Since most recipes tend to use more than one spice, it can be hard to know exactly what role each one plays and how to get the most out of it. Once you get to know them, you can break free from the recipes in this book and be as creative as you like in the kitchen.

Before you start

Make sure you have a proper clear-out. Jostle out any old ground spices that are festering in the back of the cupboard with ancient expiration dates, as they'll probably taste like sawdust and are unlikely to make anyone a decent meal.

Whole versus ground spices

The flavor of each spice comes from the oils contained in the seeds, so to get the most out of them it's a good idea to use freshly ground whole spices. But equally, if you buy small quantities on a frequent basis, pre-ground spices are fine, too. Depending on how often you're going to cook Indian food, it's actually helpful to have both whole and ground forms of coriander, cumin, black pepper, and cinnamon, as they are all regularly used in this book.

Whole spices tend to be used either to infuse oil at the start of cooking or to lend their aroma to rice. Ground spices tend to hog the limelight either individually or alongside other spices, so you need to be more careful with how you use them. Use them little by little, stirring and tasting until your food tastes the way you want it to.

Whichever you buy, make sure to store them in an airtight container like a masala dabba (a spice tin), individual jars, or even in little plastic bags in a biscuit tin.

Amchur

Dried mango powder

Amchur is a powder made from dried unripe green mangoes. As the fruit is not yet ripe, the flavor is sharp, sour, and eye-opening. It's mainly used on savory snacks such as pakoras or kebabs, to give them an extra tangy taste.

Small boxes of amchur are available online and from Indian grocers. Once opened, use within 6 months; if the powder is past its best, its flavor will be dull and it will no longer smell fragrant.

Black pepper

Mari

Kingdoms once rose and fell in the quest to obtain this "black gold" which predates the use of the chili in India, introduced in the fifteenth century by Portuguese explorers. Native to the Malabar Coast in India, pepper starts life as a vibrant green berry and is juicy, fresh, and punchy. Pick a pocket of them, leave them for a few days and they will dry into wrinkly black shot, with the fruity, woody, warm, and earthy taste for which the spice is famed. Its heat is different from that of the fresh red chili, which is more upfront and immediate.

As a main component of the spice mix garam masala (see page 267) it is responsible for making many of the beautifully warming curries in this book, such as the lamb biryani on page 118. However, it's also a winner when used in ice cream (see page 238), where the fruity notes outshine the heat.

Peppercorns are often infused into oil at the start of a dish; they soften during cooking, becoming palatable to eat (although you may prefer to push them to one side on your plate). I rarely use pre-ground pepper as I prefer to bash peppercorns up using a mortar and pestle or a spice grinder; they taste far fresher that way. You can keep peppercorns in an airtight jar in the pantry for up to 12 months.

Cardamom, green and black

Elaichi

On first sniff, cardamom smells like the perfumed older aunt of Vicks VapoRub: sweetly rosy with a touch of eucalyptus. But once you extract and crush the seeds from the pods, their aroma and flavor change into something more powerfully intense: peppery, gingery, and throat-catchingly delicious.

When finely ground and used in creams and sweets, green cardamom is transformative, brightening the other flavors and adding an elegant dimension to your food. In savory dishes, it brushes along nicely with ground black pepper, cinnamon, cumin, and cloves in garam masala (see page 267), for example. Black cardamom pods are much bigger beasts than their green counterparts and smell like bonfires and barbecue sauce, largely because they are dried over open flames. Their smoky flavor is perfect in hearty lamb curries.

To extract the seeds, bash a few pods at a time with a rolling pin or pinch them open, like a bag of chips. Grind the seeds as finely as you can with either a tiny pinch of salt or sugar, depending on the dish. When experimenting, add a pinch or two of ground cardamom until you can just taste it, as the flavor will deepen over time.

Green cardamom pods are available in most supermarkets, but you can find both ground green cardamom and black cardamom pods in Indian grocers' shops or online. Ground cardamom can be kept for 6 months or so in the pantry; as with any powder, a sniff and a lick are the best ways to determine whether the spice is still potent. The pods can be kept for up to 12 months.

Chaat masala

"Chaat" means "lick" in Hindi, and that's exactly what this mix of sprinkling spices makes you want to do to the food you've just put it on. Chaat masala contains amchur (dried mango powder), cumin, black salt, coriander, dried ginger, black pepper, and chili powder. Together they make a zingy, spicy team, covering all the basic tastes: sweet, sour, salty, and bitter.

Shake it on street food like spiced potato tikki (see page 46), papadum chaat (see page 43), garlic chicken chaat (see page 93), chapati chips (see page 272), and even fruit salads, and most definitely try it as a seasoning on home-made popcorn. Don't shake it on curries or your cereal, though. You can buy online or from an Indian grocer.

Chili powder

Marcha nu bhuko

I tend to use a blended Kashmiri chili powder, which has a mild heat and a lovely brick-red color. Whichever chili powder you use, it can become a solid and reliable friend once you get to know its potency. It can be used raw or cooked to add a consistent bite to a dish.

Use red chili powder cautiously when adding it to a dish for the first time. Add ¼ teaspoon at a time, stir, and cook for a couple of minutes before seeing if you'd like more heat.

Chili powder is available universally, so look for one with a good red color. If you store your powder in an airtight jar inside a cupboard to prolong its potency, it will keep from 3 to 6 months.

Cinnamon

Taj

Tall, dark, and handsome, cinnamon is the George Clooney of spices. True cinnamon is native to Sri Lanka, which produces 80 to 90 percent of the world's total cinnamon crop. Much of what we think of as cinnamon is actually cassia, a Chinese relative. You can tell the difference between the two by taking a close look at them: true cinnamon has tight, thin curls, often only 1/16-inch thick, whereas cassia has much thicker folds.

Cinnamon comes in two forms: sticks and ground. Sticks undoubtedly look more cheffy and will infuse rice and other dishes with a delicate flavor, whereas the ground spice is best used when you need more potency and you want to control how much flavor you're adding.

Cinnamon is great in both savory and sweet dishes. I love it alongside lamb and tomatoes (see the Howrah Express cinnamon lamb curry on page 108), or blended into a luxurious lamb biryani (see page 118). It's also one of the main components in chai masala (see page 267) and the lead spice in garam masala (see page 267). As for desserts, a few of my personal favorites are cinnamon ice cream (see page 240) and love cake (see page 233).

When buying it, look for the true Sri Lankan cinnamon and store both the sticks and the ground spice in separate airtight containers, away from sunlight. Cinnamon sticks will keep for 2 to 3 years and ground cinnamon will keep for up to 12 months.

Cloves

Loving

You know Christmas has arrived when the cloves come out. Just as these spice buds give a belly-warming feeling to English food in the deep midwinter, they add a good depth of flavor to Indian food all year round.

Known as "loving" in Gujarati, cloves are the ultimate natural antiseptic and antioxidant – I grew up using them for toothache and stomach aches. They are also one of the main components of the frequently used spice mix garam masala (see page 267). Be careful, though: just a pinch of the ground spice, or 4 or so cloves, will be enough to impart a gentle flavor without being overpowering.

They are best used whole to infuse the oil at the start of a dish. You can grind them to release their oils, but be prepared to put some elbow grease into it as they're as tough as nails.

Cloves can be bought easily, both whole and ground, and stored for up to 6 months. Look for cloves with large, circular, intact heads.

Coriander seeds and ground coriander

Dhana

These little balloon-like orbs smell gorgeous and taste citrusy and woody, with tiny hints of flowers and basil. Both coriander seeds and ground coriander are essential as an everyday spice in Indian cooking; ground coriander forms half of one of the most popular spice mixes within Indian cooking, dhana-jiru, the other half of which is ground cumin.

To get the best out of the seeds, toast them for 1 to 2 minutes on a high heat in a dry frying pan, then crush them. They are delicious with red peppers and paneer (see page 76) and Bombay eggs (see page 145), and add a lovely floral note to chicken and coriander samosas (see page 51).

Although fresh coriander is called cilantro, you can't substitute either the ground or the seed forms for the fresh cilantro leaves. Both the whole and the ground spice are widely available. Grinding the seeds yourself will produce a fresher and tastier spice than the pre-ground variety, but if you buy the latter make sure you do so in small quantities and replace it regularly. Store both the seeds and the ground spice in airtight containers. The seeds will keep for 2 years and the powder for 6 months.

1. Mace 2. Fenugreek leaves 3. Cloves
4. Sev 5. Cardamom (green) 6. Green chilis
7. Star anise 8. Green mangoes 9. Fennel seeds

2.

3.

5.

6.

8.

9.

Cumin seeds and ground cumin

Jiru

Cumin is the most hardworking spice in the cupboard and the base note to a lot of curries. It often gets partnered with coriander, which brings a happy shine to cumin's warm, burnt-toast flavor. Cumin seeds are thin, long, and striped green and brown. When roasted, they become darker, pungent, nutty, and smoky. There are black cumin seeds, too, which have a smokier and more elegant flavor and are often used in biryanis.

Cumin is an all-rounder and is found in many recipes, but it works particularly well with lamb, as in lamb kebabs (see page 109), and with butter and cheese, for example in chili paneer (see page 27). The seeds can be used to infuse oil at the start of cooking or to add fragrance to rice, and the ground spice is often used alongside other spices to add a strong and comforting flavor.

Both forms of the spice are readily available. Store them separately in airtight containers and use the powder within 3 months.

Fennel seeds

Valiary

These pale green torpedo-shaped seeds taste a little like sweet licorice and anise but are less pungent, so are refreshing when used in fennel seed ice cream (see page 243) and also make a great addition to cookies (see page 231).

They are used in savory Indian dishes, too, complementing the sweetness of pork and fish particularly well, and are found most commonly in the Bengali spice mix "panch phoran." If you've been to an Indian restaurant or two, you've no doubt also been offered fennel in the shape of "mukwas," an after-dinner digestive consisting of fennel, dill, caraway, sesame, and coriander seeds, roasted with salt, turmeric, and lemon juice.

Always buy the seeds rather than the ground form. Dry-roasting the seeds in a frying pan brings out their nutty flavor; just swirl them around in a medium-hot pan for a couple of minutes until they turn a shade darker, then bash the roasted seeds up using a mortar and pestle to release more flavor. They can be found easily and kept in an airtight container for 6 months or so in the pantry.

Fenugreek seeds and leaves

Methi

Fenugreek seeds are mostly responsible for the smell that emanates from generic storebought curry powder. They are tan-colored, small, and rigid, and look like they've been fashioned from ceramic. Nutty and crunchy, they have a shockingly bitter aftertaste, which means they should never be used on their own, only among other robust flavors and in small quantities. They're often used in pickles to add a bitter note and balance, but after some time soaking in a pickle they become softer and milder. The leaves are small and pear-shaped. Although they look like pea shoots, they are more robust and can be identified by their strong smell, like a curry-house kitchen.

The seeds are known for their powerful antiviral properties, which means Gujarati cooks tend to use them at the start of dishes, when they are thrown into hot oil alongside mustard seeds. The leaves are earthy and potent and taste great with lamb (methi gosht) and stuffed into parathas. Although the leaves are harder to come by, they are fun to experiment with, especially since their smell can be found on your skin a day after eating.

The seeds can be bought in the spice section of supermarkets and will keep for years in an airtight container. The leaves can be bought in big bunches online or from larger supermarkets and Indian grocers, and will keep for 1 to 2 days in the fridge.

1. Nutmeg 2. Ground turmeric 3. Mustard seeds 4. Chili flakes 5. Cinnamon 6. Cardamom (black) 7. Tamarind 8. Peanuts 9. Coriander seeds

2.

3.

5.

6.

8.

9.

Garam masala

"Garam" means "hot" – but in this case hot means "body-warming" rather than "spicy" – and "masala" is a general term for "mix." Every Indian woman has her own garam masala spice mix, which makes her home cooking unique, and each mix is normally a closely guarded secret and never usually discussed (unless you happen to be writing a book on Indian food).

Garam masala can include all sorts of warming spices; however, my mum's favorites are cinnamon, black pepper, and cloves – in that order – and I have given her recipe on page 267. When there is a nip in the air, you can use a small amount to add warmth to a dish towards the end of cooking. It is very good in meat dishes, especially with lamb – see the Howrah Express cinnamon lamb curry, page 108; lamb biryani, page 118 – and is also great with chickpeas, such as in the workers' curry on page 173.

Make it in a spice grinder or a coffee grinder. If you're not able to make your own, you can buy it, but choose a good-quality brand, such as Jalpur Millers.

Mustard seeds

Rai

Black mustard seeds are the original snap, crackle, and pop. Most Gujaratis throw these little seeds into hot oil at the start of a dish, which looks like magical wizardry because they start to pop furiously. They have a lovely toasted nutty flavor and are used in many dishes as an all-rounder, but are most delicious when used with fish and seafood, for example in jumbo shrimp with garlic and mustard seeds (see page 138). You could also crush the seeds to make a coarse mustard paste, and slather it over your fish before cooking, as the Bengalis do.

Look for big black mustard seeds. They can be stored in an airtight jar for up to a year.

Nutmeg

Jaifur

Sweet, nutty, and strong, nutmeg has spiced up foods for hundreds of years. Native to the Molucca Islands (or Spice Islands) of Indonesia, it grows on an evergreen tree as a small fruit; the spice mace grows around it like a lacy coat.

Nutmeg in Indian cooking is used as it is in English cooking: predominantly to perk up a dessert. Grate it over a fig firni (see page 226), into a love cake (see page 233), or over Sanjay's spiced hot chocolate (see page 253). Make sure that you buy whole nutmegs and store them in a lidded jar, where they will keep for a year or so.

Saffron

Kesar

It takes the stamens of 80,000 crocus flowers to get just 1 pound of saffron: it is the Chanel of the spice world – one of the most expensive ingredients you can buy. Its flavor is delicate and elegant – but the longer you give it to infuse into a dish, the more it will give you back both in flavor and in color. It is a complex and transformative spice, tasting a little of grass, hay, and honey.

To get the most out of saffron, steep it for a few minutes in a couple of tablespoons of hot water or milk to draw out its flavor and color, then drizzle it into rice or your chosen dish. Because it is such an expensive and delicate ingredient, I use it when it has the potential to shine. Indian cooks say Kashmiri or Iranian saffron is the best, although Spanish saffron is more widely available. All these can be used, but if going to an Indian grocer, be sure to add saffron to your shopping list.

Turmeric, fresh and ground

Hurder

Fresh turmeric is knobbly and ugly, like Gollum's feet, but scratch the surface with your fingernail and its blinding carrot-orange root unfurls beneath. It will stain everything in sight: your fingers, the dog, the tables, and place mats (which is why I use only yellow place mats these days). It has numerous health benefits, ranging from antioxidant and antiviral to anti-carcinogenic and anti-inflammatory, and unsurprisingly is also used as a food coloring and a dye.

Fresh turmeric tastes earthy, peppery, and faintly bitter. For the most part, we use the primary-colored ground turmeric in our cooking. Turmeric rarely plays a starring role in the line-up of ingredients, but it does add an earthiness.

Look for fresh turmeric which has a smooth tight skin, and try to buy bigger pieces, which will be easier to process. As for the ground spice, look for an orange-yellow powder with a strong smell. Put the powder into an airtight container and store out of direct sunlight, where it'll keep for up to a year.

Fresh herbs and leaves

Cilantro

Lila dhana

Contrary to popular practice, cilantro—fresh coriander leaves—is not needed to garnish every single curry. But as it is a bright, citrusy herb which is best friends with lemon, tomato, and garlic, it does make a welcome and fresh addition to many dishes in Indian cooking.

Cilantro will wilt and lose its flavor when thrown into a pan, so it's best scattered on top of dishes or stirred in at the last minute, just before serving. Its crowning glory is a bright and delicious cilantro chutney (see page 212), where the cilantro mixes perfectly with creamy peanuts, sharp lemon, chili, and sugar. Unlike other fresh herbs, both the leaves and the stalks can and should be used in cooking, although cilantro leaves cannot be substituted for coriander seeds or ground coriander.

The best way to buy it is in big bunches from the farmers' market, where it is cheap, fresh, and will still have its roots attached. Don't worry about any grit: you can dunk your bunch of cilantro into a large bowl of water, give it a shake, pull it out, and leave it to dry in a sieve. Any dirt will fall to the bottom of the bowl and you'll be left with clean sprightly leaves. To store, first remove any yellow or brown leaves, then wrap it in paper towels, and pop it in the fridge.

Curry leaves

Limbro

Curries don't grow on trees, but curry leaves do. Also known as sweet neem leaves, they are a bright, shiny dark green and look a bit like bay leaves. They smell potently of sweet pepper and tangerine, taste divine, and impart a smoky lemony flavor to dishes.

I mostly use them at the start of cooking. By quickly brushing your hand up the twig, you can release all the leaves at once into some hot oil, where they will crackle fiercely (be careful) and infuse the oil with their flavor. They are wonderful in the simple but delicious coconut fish curry on page 127 and in the mussels in a coconut and ginger sauce on page 134. Alternatively, they can be used in a tarka, which is an infusion of spices in oil, used to dress dal and ondwa (see page 35).

They can occasionally be bought fresh in big supermarkets, and easily online or from Indian grocers. Look for bright, shiny, and unmarked leaves. They can be kept in a plastic bag in the fridge for a week, up to a year when dried, or up to 6 months in the freezer. I prefer to use frozen leaves rather than dried, although both lack the intensity of the fresh leaves.

Dill leaves and seeds

Sua

Sweet, grassy dill, with its emerald fern-like leaves, is not sidelined in Indian cooking, but used boldly as a vegetable and cooked as though it were spinach. It works like a charm when cooked with potatoes, but it can equally be used uncooked to lift dishes, and works especially well alongside lemon. I like to use it with rice

(see page 158) and in wild mushroom pilau (see page 170), and it makes for a good addition to raita, too. Both leaves and stalks can be used.

Dill seeds are small, flat, and tear-shaped, with a pale brown edge and a mahogany center, and are also used in Indian cooking. They smell faintly of camphor, taste similar to caraway seeds and aniseed, and are often used by Gujarati mothers to cure colic in babies.

To store, sprinkle paper towels with some cold water, loosely wrap the dill in it, and store in the fridge, where it should keep for 2 to 5 days.

Mint leaves

Fodino

Fresh mint adds a bright and invigorating dimension to Indian food and works well with lots of other flavors, although my favorites of its many partners are cilantro and coconut (see fish in a cilantro, coconut, and mint parcel, page 137). Its cooling properties are also very welcome in chutneys (see page 219) and raitas (see page 188) and as an addition to ginger cordial (see page 252) and lime soda (see page 250). Dried mint is rarely used in the Indian kitchen.

Buy the freshest-looking leaves you can find, with no black spots, and store them in the fridge, wrapped in paper towels sprinkled with water. As with cilantro and dill, colossal bunches can be bought much more cheaply from Indian grocers or farmers' markets than at the supermarket.

Legumes and grains

Grains and legumes are the foundation of most of India's meals. Endless combinations of these cheap pantry ingredients make for nourishing, magnificent meals. Although many beans and lentils are available in canned form, ideal for a quick meal, their dried counterparts, which require some soaking and boiling, are more delicious if you have the time. Rather happily, most dried grains, legumes, and lentils can be stored for

a year, if not longer, in airtight containers, making them a great staple to keep in the kitchen.

Legumes

Black lentils

Urad dal

Black lentils, or urad dal, are diamonds in the rough. Give them time and they will reward you handsomely with their rich, smoky flavor and creamy texture. Surprisingly, they keep their shape, too, even after hours of cooking.

It's best to use them whole, particularly in dal makhani (see page 167), where they're cooked in milk until they create one of the finest dals known to mankind. It's unlikely you'll find black lentils in your local supermarket, so you'll need to forage online or at your local Indian grocer's shop to get hold of them.

Chana dal

Split chickpea lentils

Chana dal are the most naturally flavorful of the lentil family as they are the split halves of the black chickpea. They are bigger and more knobbly-looking than the smoother, smaller yellow lentil, and nutty in flavor. As they lose their shape a little when cooked, they will leave you with a luscious thick dal with some bite.

You can buy them in some larger supermarkets, online, or from Indian grocers.

Chickpeas, black and white

Chana and kala chana

These ancient legumes, which were first cultivated thousands of years ago, still fill the bellies of millions of Indians in the form of chana masala, a rich, spicy, and creamy chickpea stew (see the workers' curry on page 173). Chickpeas start life as the fresh green seeds of a bush and are then dried to form the hard white chickpeas we know. Black chickpeas, kala chana, are smaller, harder, and darker than their white cousin. They have a musky, nutty flavor and a thicker skin and are now gaining a presence on the shelves of our larger supermarkets.

There is a big difference between using dried and canned white chickpeas. Canned white chickpeas can be chalky, but dried chickpeas which have been soaked and boiled are voluptuous and creamy. You'll need to soak them for 6 to 8 hours and cook them for a further 45 minutes. Canned chickpeas can be used to make one of India's ultimate snacks, chana ka chips – crispy spiced chickpeas (see page 40). Black chickpeas can be bought in cans and don't need to be soaked and cooked – just rinse and drain them.

You can buy white chickpeas, both dried and canned, from most supermarkets. Stored properly, they last for a couple of years. Black chickpeas can be bought in the "world food" section of larger supermarkets or from Indian grocers.

Kidney beans
Junjaro (Gujarati) or rajma (Hindi)

These ruby-red beans taste their best when soaked in water overnight (or for 8 hours), then boiled until cooked. Because of their natural earthy flavor and heavy texture they work well with the warming spices in garam masala: cinnamon, cloves, and black pepper.

Buy bright, shiny dried kidney beans, or, if time-poor, good-quality canned kidney beans. Make sure to rinse and drain canned kidney beans before using them, and check whether they're in salted water before adding salt to your meal.

Mung beans and split mung beans
Moong dal

You might be forgiven for thinking that these were the tiny moss-colored green beans that good old Jack was given to grow his beanstalk from. Plant them in some warm water and they quickly turn into one of India's greatest superfoods, bean sprouts, which are rich in protein and

highly nutritious. See page 271 for how to sprout your own.

As sprouts they are fresh, crunchy, and surprisingly substantial, and they make for one of my favorite summer meals: sprouted beans with garlic, lemon, and cumin (see page 83). I also like to throw them into salads, such as my papadum chaat (see page 43). When split in half, mung beans are white and the star legume in the ancient rice dish kitchari (see page 159).

More often than not, you'll be able to find mung beans in the supermarket. Store securely in their bag or in an airtight container.

Pigeon peas, or yellow split peas
Toor dal

Toor are small, smooth, and circular, smaller than chana dal, and take longer to cook than their red counterparts. They seldom lose their shape, which is good if you prefer your dal with a bit more texture. They frequently form the base of the classic Gujarati dal (simply called toor dal), and sambhar, a sweet and sour dish eaten every day in the south of India.

They are readily available in their dried form in supermarkets, or as "oily toor dal," covered in a fine layer of oil. I'd recommend using dry over oily as the latter have to be soaked in hot water, washed, and boiled just to remove the oil.

Red lentils
Masoor dal

Red lentils are the people's choice: the crowd-pleasers and the quick-cookers. Although they start life as whole brown-colored lentils, they are skinned and split to reveal their blazing orange insides. These lentils are a household staple across the whole of India and are most often used in India's most comforting dish, dal (see pages 162–7).

Red lentils are perfect for a quick dinner as they cook in just 20 minutes without any prior soaking.

After cooking they lose their shape, giving a thick soupy texture. They need to be partnered with some bold flavors and work well with garlic, browned onions, slow-cooked tomatoes, or even coconut milk.

You can buy them from supermarkets or in larger quantities from Indian grocers.

Rice

Basmati rice

Bhat

While there are over 250 types of rice grown in India, basmati is considered the best. This is partly due to its long, elegant, silky grains, which separate into fluffy individual grains when cooked, and also because of its delicate flavor, which makes it great to eat by itself with a pat of butter and a few cloves or other spices (see the cinnamon, clove, and cashew pilau on page 156).

Basmati rice is widely available. Stored in a secured bag or airtight container basmati rice has an almost indefinite shelf life.

Poha

Beaten rice flakes

Poha is the name given to pre-cooked and beaten rice flakes; in short, it's rice without the fuss. In our family home, poha is eaten for breakfast, lunch, or as a hefty snack alongside potatoes, peanuts, chilies, lemon juice, cilantro, and coconut (see page 161). Poha is never used with sauces as it would disintegrate. To cook it, you need only dunk it in water briefly, drain it, and put it into a pan, then cover and steam it for a minute or so until just cooked.

There are fine, medium, and thick grades of poha. Go for the medium, check the bag to ensure the poha flakes are largely unbroken, and watch out for the shelf life.

Flours

Chapati flour

Rotli nu lot

We use this flour to make our daily bread, the chapati. Although it's whole-grain flour, it's more finely milled than the regular whole-grain flour you'll find in supermarkets. If you can't get ahold of it, you can use equal parts of normal whole-grain flour and white flour instead.

The chapati may be the world's easiest bread to make. There's no yeasting, no resting, no raising, no baking. The flour can also be used to make puris (small balloons of fried bread); paratha (see page 198); and thepla (see page 275), which are flavorsome Gujarati flatbreads.

Chapati flour is sometimes called "atta," and can often be found in the "world food" section of supermarkets; if not, it will be in your local Indian grocer's shop. Stored in an airtight container, it should keep for 6 to 8 months.

Chickpea flour, or gram flour

Chana nu lot, or besan

A naturally tasty savory flour which is made from roasted and ground chickpeas, it can be used to make pancakes (known as "pudlas"; see page 207) or a simple light sauce for okra called "kadhi" (see page 73). Beyond this book, there are another thousand uses for it, in snacks such as sev (chickpea noodles), fursan, ghantia, and bhajia (fried chickpea snacks), and dhokla (a delicious spongy snack). It's best used on its own in sauces and as a batter, but occasionally needs to be mixed with other flour or rising agents to stop it from becoming too dense and sticky.

It's a joyful surprise that chickpea flour is now available in the "world food" section of most supermarkets, where it may be called "besan." If you tightly secure the paper bag it comes in with a bag clip and store it out of direct sunlight, the flour should last up to 18 months.

Millet flour

Bajra nu lot

Millet has been cultivated in India for the last 10,000 years and grows readily in Gujarat, making this flour one of the most common bread flours there. It has a shorter shelf life than ordinary flour, along with an incredible ability to imitate wet cement when mixed with water. Nevertheless, it's one of my favorite flours. Millet flatbreads have an earthy and ancient flavor – how I imagine some of the first breads ever made would have tasted.

My grandma layers them up in a tight vessel with fresh young garlic shoots, oil, and salt and lets them steam in the heat of the bread, before breaking up the mixture into large crumbs with a flat palette knife. Called "lasan nu rotlo," this is my mother's favorite dish. I make a much simpler version on page 203. Millet flatbreads also go well with homemade white butter and jaggery.

You can buy this flour online or from Indian grocers; just be sure to keep it in an airtight container. The quality of millet flour does vary; I always taste the flour before using. Old or spoiled millet flour will taste acrid.

Rice flour

Bhat nu lot

Rice flour is made from raw ground rice and can be used as a thickener or to make batters or breads (like the wonderful South Indian dosa). I use it to make a smooth, sweet rice pudding called "firni," which I love to eat with a dollop of fig jam (see page 226). Many supermarkets sell their own brand, which you can find in the rice aisle. If you store it in an airtight container, it should last up to 18 months.

Semolina

Sooji

Don't be surprised if an Indian crosses your palm with a dollop of semolina cooked in ghee and sugar when you're at an Indian temple or religious ceremony. It's usually used as an offering to Indian deities, then blessed and offered to all as a rich, sweet, and soothing gift.

Its wheat origin and size make it a versatile ingredient in Indian cooking, but I mainly use coarse semolina to make ondwa, the famous savory vegetable-lined Gujarati snack (see page 35), and fine semolina to make a sweet love cake (see page 233), which gives it a lovely dense texture. It is widely available.

Vegetables and roots

Cassava (or tapioca)

Mogo

The use of cassava in Indian cooking is specific to the East African Asian community, predominantly to make beautiful chili fries (mogo ni chips). Bad cassava are black inside; good ones are white.

Make the fries by cutting the cassava into 2½-inch blocks and peeling off the skin. Pop them into cold water to soak while you bring a pan of salted water to a boil. Boil the cassava until soft, then put a fine layer of oil in a hot frying pan and shallow-fry them for around 6 minutes, turning every 2 minutes. Sprinkle with chili powder, salt, and a squeeze of lemon, and eat quickly.

You can buy cassava from Indian grocers or some outdoor vegetable markets. Store in a dry area away from sunlight, and eat within 3 to 4 days.

Chilis, fresh green and red

Lila mircha, lal mircha

Unlike the fatter chilis used in Mexican cooking or the tiny bird's-eye variety used in Thai cooking, those used in Indian cooking are long, slim, and green, and are often called "Indian" or "finger chilis." Indian chilis are green because they are unripe. That makes them hotter than their ripened red friends, but they also taste much fresher.

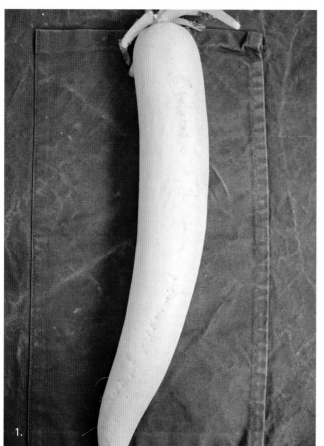

Left page, clockwise

1. Daikon
2. Bitter gourd
3. Cassava

Right page, left column

4. Chana dal
5. Split mung beans
6. Yellow split peas

Right page, right column

7. Mung beans
8. Red lentils
9. Black lentils

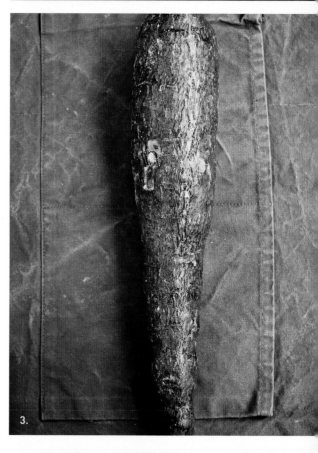

4.

5.

6.

7.

8.

9.

It's easy to figure out how much fresh chili you like by using a quarter of a chili (seeds in), finely chopped, no matter how much is stated in the recipe. If you can take more, add another quarter of the chili, and so on, before it becomes too hot to handle. Indians always eat chilis with the seeds in, as they contain most of the heat, but if you prefer you could seed your chili, or even prick a whole chili with a knife in a few places and remove it before serving. You can use fresh green chilis alongside red chili powder.

Look for bright green fresh chilis with similarly green tops. Store them wrapped in paper towels in the vegetable drawer of the fridge, where they will keep for 1 to 2 weeks.

Garlic
Lasan

Garlic is a near deity in India. Along with ginger and green chilis, it is the third key ingredient in Indian home cooking. Many Indian home cooks (my mother included) create a fresh paste of this trio, freezing it and using it whenever they need to. Garlic is used not only for its flavor but also for its anti-fungal and antibacterial properties, as well as helping to prevent colds.

Garlic is most often used near the start of cooking to give it time to flavor a dish, but sometimes it is used in oil or ghee in the final stage of a dish, for example in the chana dal with golden garlic tarka (see page 162).

To make my mum's paste, use a per-dish ratio of 4 cloves of garlic, 1¾-inch piece of of ginger, and 1 to 1½ green chilis, then scale up to your required quantity, process in a blender, and freeze in a plastic container until needed.

Fresh garlic will be dense and firm, so make sure you give the bulbs a little squeeze before you buy them, and look out for ones with nice large cloves, which will make peeling and cutting quicker and easier. Young garlic shoots can be bought from Indian grocers from around March to July.

Ginger
Adu

In Indian cooking, ginger is a steady and solid performer. It's generally added to a dish early on, which ensures that the refreshing heat subsides but also lifts the spices which follow.

Ginger is excellent with cumin, coriander, cloves, and cinnamon, but it also works really well with tomatoes, lemon, coconut, and fish. In its dried form, it's a major component of chai masala (see page 267). Although ginger rarely plays a starring role in a dish, that's not to say it can't. It's perfect in ice cream, and ginger cordial (see page 252) is a firm family favorite. I often grate it into chai to kick a cold or help with digestion.

Few people peel ginger well. The best way to ensure you lose as few of the nutrients as possible from the outer later is to peel it with a teaspoon. Hold the ginger in one hand and scrape with the top of the spoon with the other. When it comes to chopping, think about the mouthful you want when you eat the final dish. If you'd prefer not to bite into chunks of ginger, create a paste using a mortar and pestle or spice grinder. If you don't mind a spicy punch every now and then, finely dice it or grate it.

When buying ginger, look for hard, heavy, thick stems which might snap easily and avoid dry-looking, shriveled pieces. Store in the vegetable section of the fridge, where it will keep for 1 to 2 weeks.

Daikon (mooli)

Daikon, or mooli, is a giant javelin spear of pure white radish which can grow up to a meter long. Once peeled, it is wonderful raw and has a good peppery bite which is a little milder than some of the hotter English radishes I've tasted. It goes very well in a refreshing salad along with sweet carrots, crunchy red cabbage, and a chili and lime dressing (see Jaipur slaw, page 182). Outside of the salad world, it is also used to stuff paratha and beef up dals. It's great value: given its huge size, you definitely get more mooli for your money.

Buy the freshest, whitest, firmest daikon radish you can find. If it has leaves, look for the shiniest ones and use it as quickly as possible as it will wither in just a couple of days.

Okra
Bhinda

Also known as "ladies' fingers," long, star-shaped okra are a popular vegetable that pop up on many an Indian menu. When cooked in liquid they can be a bit slimy, but a few simple tricks will help.

First, don't wash them before cooking; instead, wipe them if necessary with barely damp paper towels to avoid soaking them with excess water. Secondly, sauté them on a high heat and in small batches, as this will allow them to crisp up nicely. Thirdly, throw them into any sauce right at the last minute, just before serving.

Look for firm small okra with unblemished, bright green hats. Store in the fridge and eat within a couple of days of buying.

Onions
Dungree

Although onions need little introduction, it is worth noting this golden rule: never compromise on the cooking time. A lot of the flavor in curries comes from onions, so be sure to cook them until they are soft enough to cut with a blunt wooden spoon and turn a lush rich brown at the edges.

Red onions and shallots are used raw in salads such as papadum chaat (see page 43) and kachumbar (see page 185). The key is to chop them as finely as you can, using your sharpest knife.

When using white onions in everyday dishes, make sure you buy them as large and as hard as cricket balls. Store them in a dry place outside of direct sunlight and heat and they can last up to a couple of weeks.

Plantains
Matoke

These green bananas were adopted by the Indians who went over to Uganda and other parts of East Africa (largely from Gujarat), where they grow in great swathes. Unlike bananas, plantains need to be cooked before eating. More often than not they are turned into a beautiful silky mash alongside onions, garlic, ginger, chilis, and tomatoes to make matoke (see page 70). The Ugandans often throw stock and ground beef into their version of the dish, or fry the vegetable as an accompaniment to meat.

You can find them in Caribbean and Indian grocers' shops and possibly the odd vegetable market. Use them within a week.

Fruit
Coconut and coconut milk

Naryal nu doodh

The coconut plays a vital role in both Indian religion and Indian cooking. It is offered up in prayer in temples, and in Gujarat it is customary for the bride to present her new husband with a coconut as a symbol to convey that, no matter the circumstance, they will be as strong as the coconut shell yet remain as sweet as the flesh inside.

Coconut can be used in many ways. Desiccated coconut is perfect for sweets (see the coconut-milk fudge on page 228). As for curries, like most people I take a short cut by using canned coconut milk instead of making my own. As canned coconut milk is designed more for Thai and Vietnamese cooking, I like to dilute it by using 3 parts coconut milk to 1 part water, which gives a truer taste for Indian cooking.

You can also use milk made from desiccated coconut. Just add 5 ounces of coconut to 2 cups of boiling water, leave it to steep, and cool for around an hour, then blend and strain through a cheesecloth and use within 2 days. If you want to make your own coconut milk from the flesh, it's a little bit of work but it is rewarding. Crack open a coconut by hitting it hard, all the way around its circumference, using a heavy knife or cleaver. Wedge the flesh out using a knife, put it in a food processor along with 2 cups of warm water, and blitz. Leave it to soak for an hour, then strain it through a fine-mesh sieve or a cheesecloth and use within 2 days.

Canned coconut milk and desiccated coconut are widely available, and fresh coconuts can be bought fairly cheaply from big supermarkets. Make sure you buy dark brown coconuts and give them a shake – the heavier the better, as this indicates a good, healthy, water-laden fruit. Store both the fresh coconut and canned milk in a jar or airtight container in the fridge and use within 2 to 3 days.

Mangoes

Keri

Over 300 varieties of mangoes, of different sizes and shapes, are grown in India. What's available in the West really only scratches the surface because mango season is all too brief and they bruise easily, making them difficult to transport. Those you can find all year round in supermarkets are most likely to be from Brazil and are very different from their Indian cousins.

Without a doubt, the king of the mangoes, perfuming any room when ripe, is the Alphonso mango, which is buttery, sweet, and fleshy, but, if you can't find it, keep an eye out for the Kesar mango (saffron mango), or even the Pakistani Honey mango, available a bit later in the season. All can be eaten just as they are or with a squeeze of lime. They have a green exterior, are rock solid (which makes them good for grating), and have a sour bite to them.

If, like me, you end up buying too many Alphonso mangoes, make a gorgeous sorbet out of them (see page 246), or a mango and cardamom lassi (see page 256). If you want to make Gujarati mango chutney (see page 215), look for very

hard green Rajapuri mangoes. If you head to your local Indian grocer in mango season (April to June) and ask around, you will most likely strike gold. Some online retailers are starting to provide Alphonso mangoes in season, and some supermarkets even stock a few boxes. If you buy mangoes in a box, keep them in it but take the lid off so they can ripen. Eat as quickly as you can once ripe.

Pomegranates

Daram

My grandma used to sit us down as children with a pomegranate to seed to keep us out of mischief. The sweet ruby-red jewels were mesmerizing to me as a little girl, and even now they have the ability to add charm and delight to a meal, working well with both sweet and savory dishes. It's worth noting that seeding pomegranates the wrong way can result in the kitchen looking like a crime scene. Below is the clean, easy, and graceful way to do it – it should only take around 5 minutes:

Step 1: take one pomegranate and a knife.

Step 2: chop the fruit into quarters.

Step 3: break each segment in half and watch the seeds pop out.

Step 4: ruffle the rest of the seeds out, using your thumbs.

You can either eat the seeds by themselves, or throw them into raitas (see the pomegranate and mint raita on page 188) or over dishes, as a garnish (see the papadum chaat on page 43). They make for a precious sprinkle over kulfi and ice cream, too, especially pistachio and saffron kulfi (see page 244) and love cake (see page 233).

When buying pomegranates, look for big, bright, rosy-red ones in the supermarket, Indian grocers' shops, or Iranian shops. You can keep them in a cool, dry place for a couple of weeks. If seeded, always refrigerate the seeds and eat within 2 to 3 days.

Cooking oils and fats

Despite the big, bold flavors that Indian cooking is known for, the oils and fats used to cook with are largely neutral in flavor to allow for the subtleties of the spices to shine through. As a general rule, all oils should be stored in a dark, cool place, out of direct sunlight.

Ghee

Clarified butter

The smell of fresh ghee makes me weak at the knees. It has huge religious and cultural significance in India, as well as being a key ingredient in Indian cooking. It is clarified butter, made by heating butter until the milk solids separate, leaving a clear and long-lasting fat which is siphoned off as ghee while the milk solids fall to the bottom of the pan.

Ghee is hugely versatile due to its high smoke point (meaning it withstands heat very well), which makes it suitable for frying. Although homemade ghee is wonderful (see the recipe on page 269), you can buy it from some larger supermarkets or Indian grocers. Removing the milk solids in butter prolongs its life, which means that ghee can be kept in an airtight jar in the cupboard for a month or two.

Peanut oil

Peanut oil is the oil my mother grew up using, as there are plenty of peanuts to make it with in Uganda and India. Sadly, it doesn't taste of peanuts, but it's perfect to use in many dishes as it's neutral in flavor and has a high smoke point.

Canola oil

This is my favorite oil and the one I use daily in my cooking because of its many attributes. It has a very subtle nutty flavour, a high smoke point, making it good for frying, and it is very low in saturated fats.

Sunflower oil

Many Indians use sunflower oil, and there's little difference in using peanut or sunflower oil. They're both light oils and solid performers, although sunflower oil is slightly lower in saturated fats than peanut oil.

Seasoning oils

Coconut oil

Coconut oil is utterly delicious. Dreamy and creamy, it's perfect for imparting a delicate flavor to fish dishes and is used predominantly in South India for cooking. It's very expensive here in the UK unless bought in an Indian grocer's shop or online, and I use it infrequently because it's not a particularly stable oil and so isn't suited to frying at high temperatures. However, a spoonful stirred into a fish curry or rice, right at the end of cooking, tastes sublime.

Mustard oil

As you can imagine, mustard oil packs a punch. An intense, amber-colored liquid, it's a fantastic oil to have in the cupboard to drizzle over fish, chicken, or salad leaves to pep them up. While it's not suitable for general cooking due to its strong flavor and unstable nature, it's a fabulous oil to dress food with and to use in pickling.

Salt and sugar

For everyday cooking I use regular table salt and sugar, although I've become partial to the flavor and texture of sea salt in recent years and love using it to grind chili, garlic, and ginger more easily with a mortar and pestle. I use black salt and jaggery more occasionally (see page 306).

Black salt

Kala namak

Black salt is mined from volcanic rock salt in Central India and, contrary to its name, is a deep ruby black when in rock form but turns pale pink when ground. It has a somewhat sulfurous taste due to its mineral content, but is lower in sodium than refined salt. A scant amount on top of sweet potato, and in chaat masala (see page 287) and raitas, makes for a tasty addition. Surprisingly, you can add it to fruit salads and mango lassis, too, for an interesting sweet and salty combination. Buy online or from Indian grocers, and you should store it as you would any other salt, away from moisture.

Jaggery

Jaggery tastes of toffee, fudge, and maple syrup. It is made by pressing sugarcane to extract the juice, which is evaporated to create a molten caramel-like syrup. This is then strained but not refined, and left to solidify. The first harvest is a cause for celebration in many villages in India, and farmers call locals to come and feast on the initial batch of jaggery – which probably causes not only happiness, but also hyper-excitability.

It comes in various grades, just like olive oils, and is used mainly in sweets. I buy a big block and chip away at it using a knife (or hammer) whenever I need it, and particularly love caramelizing it and throwing in nuts to make pistachio brittle (see page 237). My grandma used to make cough drops by rolling hot jaggery with turmeric for us to suck on when my sister or I was ill.

Good jaggery should be golden, soft, and shiny, although most Indian grocers sell hard, bowl-shaped jaggery, which isn't bad. Buy jaggery online, too. Stored in an airtight container, it should last for 4 to 5 months.

Other secret ingredients

Peanuts

Jugu

These are loved by monkeys, Indian cooks, and beer drinkers equally. I tend to buy them in large quantities, raw (rather than roasted), and with their red skins intact. I use them ground in chutneys to give texture (see the cilantro chutney on page 212), on potatoes to give bite in an aloo gobi salad (see page 74) and ferarri (see page 177), and as the main component of a rich but humble stew, Jyoti's peanut soup (see page 169).

Look for unroasted and unsalted peanuts, or roasted and unsalted, which are most likely to be hiding in the baking aisle of the supermarket and occasionally sold as monkey nuts with their shells still on. If you store them in a bag or airtight container, they'll keep for 3 to 4 months.

Rose water

Gulab nu pani

Used in moderation, rose water, made from the distilled essence of rose petals, can lend a subtle fragrance and soft sweetness to a dish. Too much can leave you feeling like you've licked a bar of soap and followed with a chaser of perfume, however, so be sparing.

Rose water is used in the summer months in India for its cooling effect, mainly in ice creams, lassis and sweets. I love it in cardamom and rose water kulfi (see page 247). All rose waters vary in their intensity, and the best advice I can give is to be gentle, adding a tablespoon at a time until you can just taste it without it being overpowering.

Supermarkets often sell both rose water and rose essence. Rose essence is created by steeping petals in alcohol, which makes for a stronger solution. Store both in their bottles away from strong sunlight.

1. Jaggery 2. Mustard oil
3. Fresh turmeric 4. Fresh coconut

1.

2.

3.

4.

Sev

Fried chickpea noodles

Sev are crunchy chickpea noodles, which feature in many different snack foods across India, most famously in Bombay mix. They're made with chickpea flour, which is turned into a stiff dough by adding water, salt, and a bit of turmeric. This is then squeezed through a press into hot oil and fried. They can be used in all sorts of street foods, such as papadum chaat (see page 43), but we also use them in a popular Gujarati curry called "sev tamatar," in which handfuls are added to a tomato curry (see page 77).

I like to use the ultra-fine "nylon sev" in most of my recipes, but the pleasingly chunky "thick sev" make for excellent crisp substitutes. Store them in an airtight container and eat in a matter of weeks.

Tamarind

Ambli

Tamarind is India's secret weapon. It has a wonderful bittersweetness to it, in the same way that a fizzy cola or fresh lemonade has, and it amply satisfies the taste buds. Tamarind starts life as a fruit, growing high up in trees, and you could be forgiven for thinking that it looks suspiciously like poo. But it adds a marvelous bite and zing to dishes and goes well with chili and honey (see roasted tamarind chicken with honey and red chili on page 94), and also with coconut (see coconut and tamarind chicken curry on page 96). It also forms the key ingredient in one of India's most popular street-food chutneys: date and tamarind chutney (see page 216). Try adding half a teaspoon of paste at a time to dal or fish curries if they need brightening up, but be careful not to add too much as tamarind can vary in its potency and turn everything sour.

It comes in many forms: in its natural fruit form, in blocks, or in generic supermarket jars. For ease, consistency, and flavor, I use tamarind paste from the jar. Once opened, store in the fridge and use within 4 weeks.

Dairy

India is the world's largest producer and consumer of milk. Indians drink it in chai (see page 260) or as lassi (see pages 256 and 259), eat it as yogurt, cook with it as ghee, stir it into curries, make cheese from it, and put it into endless desserts.

Milk

Doodh

I tend to use whole milk, purely because it doesn't curdle as easily as skim or low-fat in cooking.

Paneer

Despite India's love for dairy, it only has eyes for one cheese: paneer. It can be easily made (see page 264) or bought in supermarkets. Store-bought paneer is vaguely similar to halloumi, although it's not seasoned. The best way to treat it is to fry it evenly until golden brown before throwing it into a sauce; see my chili paneer (page 27) and my slow-cooked red pepper and paneer curry (page 76), for example. Homemade paneer is distantly related to ricotta, so it works well with other fresh flavors like peas, tomatoes, and a pinch or two of garam masala. You don't need to fry homemade paneer; as it has a delicate texture, you can just fold it into a dish.

Yogurt

Dahi

I either make my own yogurt, which is easily done (see page 266), or buy set yogurt – similar to homemade yogurt – or Greek yogurt, which is similar to our Gujarati strained yogurt (called "shrikhand" when sweetened).

Recommended suppliers

These days our supermarkets stock most of the ingredients you need for Indian home cooking, especially in the "world food" section, although I'd encourage you to seek out your local Indian grocer's shop to see what it has in store. Here are some of my favorite suppliers:

Equipment

For low-tech equipment such as rolling pins, chapati boards, large mortar and pestles, and the essential spice tin, any number of Indian grocers will stock these, but if buying online try:

Indian Blend
www.indianblend.com

For high-tech equipment such as food processors and ice cream makers:

Magimix
www.magimix.com

For a durable and brilliant spice and nut grinder:

Cuisinart
www.cuisinart.com

Oils

For mustard oil and coconut oil (most others, such as canola, peanut oil, and ghee should be available in your local supermarket):

Pure Indian Foods
www.pureindianfoods.com

Spices, legumes, and flour

For all types of spices and top-quality flour, from millet flour (bajra) to chickpea flour (besan):

Bob's Red Mill
www.bobsredmill.com

For good-quality spices:

The Spice House
www.thespicehouse.com

Savory Spice Shop
www.savoryspiceshop.com

My Spice Sage
www.myspicesage.com

INDEX

Thanks!

THANK YOU

To my fantastic mother, who raised us and fed us on the most divine food.

To both my parents, for their unconditional love and support.

To Peter Gowlett, who thought to ask me if I had a publisher (when I had never thought to publish); Briony Gowlett, who encouraged me to write the proposal for this book; and Eric Treuille at Books for Cooks, for kicking me out of his shop door and telling me to get on with it.

To Stephen Joyce, who so beautifully photographed the initial book proposal; and Chris Chapman, whose design skills never cease to amaze me.

To Richard Reed, Adam Balon, Jon Wright, and all at innocent drinks for the scholarship money which allowed me to meet my family in India and collect their recipes.

To Mahesh Multani and family, Sam Patel, Mukundmama and Hasumama Thakrar and family, for hosting and feeding me in Mumbai, Porbandar, and Rajkot.

To my grandma and all my uncles, aunts and cousins, for their stories.

To Sam and Sam Clark, Stevie Parle, and Rich Blackwell, for allowing me to work in their kitchens at Moro and the Dock Kitchen.

To Felicity Rubinstein and Jane Finigan, my fantastic agents, for giving me a chance to immortalize my family, our stories, and our recipes, and for being so supportive along the way.

To Juliet Annan and Sophie Missing, my editors, for having faith in me and helping me to turn my dream into a book, one day at a time.

To my grandma, Jyoti Patel, Raoul Ray, Sanjay Sharma, Sam Bompas, Kirti at Mirissa Hills, Rich Blackwell, Hannah Cameron McKenna, Kumari, Kirthi, Harsha Lakhani, and Harsha and Disha Thakrar, for contributing or helping me with a recipe.

To all the brave guinea pigs: Connor Cameron McKenna, Matt Maude, Simon and Kassie Darling Maude, Raoul and Bianca Ray, Julie Strilesky, Chris and Olivia Chapman, Andrew Bulger, Teresa Towner, James Hughes, Rob Kinder, Sophie Hug, Monica Niermann, Sam Trusty, Chris and Vicki Smith, Tansy Drake and Andrew Dickens, Alex Whitmore, Ted Hunt, Kalyan Karmaker, Ally McCann, and Anth Baxter, Anna and Andy Bickerdike, Peter and Rubina de Winton, and all those at innocent, graze.com, DARE, Moro, and the Dock Kitchen.

To Sue Sethi, for contributing a brilliant piece on what to drink with your meal and helping to debunk the myth that wine is wasted on Indian food.

To dear Ceridwen Tallett, for wondrous support and for rigorously ensuring the words made sense; and to Ceri's mum, Sian Tallett, for all the amazing vegetables from her allotment.

To Hannah Cameron McKenna, for meticulously testing every single recipe in the book.

To David (Lord) Loftus, for his creative genius, extraordinary photographs, and all his wonderful stories.

To John Hamilton, for making this book a very beautiful one and being so much fun to work with.

To Alison O'Toole, Sarah Fraser, Ellie Smith, Caroline Pretty, Poppy North, Alice Burkle, and everyone who has worked on the book at Penguin.

To my U.S. editor, Will Schwalbe, and the rest of the team at Flatiron Books: Bob Miller, Marlena Bittner, Liz Keenan, Bryn Clark, and Kara Rota. You've made the American Dream possible for a little girl from Lincolnshire.

To Mary Goodbody, for translating this book so that it's worthy of an American kitchen.

And finally, to Hugh, who is between every line of every page of this book.